Preparing
Children
for
Court

Interpersonal Violence:
The Practice Series

Jon R. Conte, Series Editor

Preparing
Children
for
Court

A Practitioner's Guide

Lynn M. Copen

Interpersonal Violence:
The Practice Series

Sage Publications, Inc.
International Educational and Professional Publisher
Thousand Oaks ▪ London ▪ New Delhi

For information:

Sage Publications, Inc.
2455 Teller Road
Thousand Oaks, California 91320
E-mail: order@sagepub.com

Sage Publications Ltd.
6 Bonhill Street
London EC2A 4PU
United Kingdom

Sage Publications India Pvt. Ltd.
M-32 Market
Greater Kailash I
New Delhi 110 048 India

Printed in the United States of America

Library of Congress Cataloging-in-Publication Data

Copen, Lynn M.
  Preparing children for court: A practitioner's guide / by Lynn M. Copen.
      p.   cm. — (Interpersonal violence)
Includes bibliographical references and index.
    ISBN 0-7619-2194-X (pbk.: acid-free paper)
    1. Child witnesses—United States.   I. Title.   II. Series.
    KF9673.C67   2000
    347.73'66'083—dc21   00-008184

00   01   02   03   10   9   8   7   6   5   4   3   2   1

Acquiring Editor:	Nancy Hale
Production Editor:	Diana E. Axelsen
Editorial Assistant:	Cindy Bear
Typesetter:	Janelle LeMaster
Indexer:	Teri Greenberg

Contents

APPENDIXES

Foreword

I was pleased to be asked to write a foreword for *Preparing Children for Court*. This book represents a compilation of "tricks of the trade" by a very talented victim-witness advocate, Lynn Copen. The ideas presented herein are relevant for a wide variety of professions: victim-witness advocate, therapist, court advocate, social worker, prosecutor, defense attorney, and others who have occasion to prepare children to testify in court proceedings. The ideas presented in this book not only assist professionals in doing their job competently, but also allow children to enter the legal system without incurring further damage. Proper preparation allows the court system to seek what is intended—the truth—from adult and child witnesses alike.

As you read this book, you will notice the underlying assumption that children are quite competent to be credible witnesses in court proceedings when prepared properly. This preparation does *not* mean rote rehearsal of case facts. The preparation involves equipping children to enter the justice system, to understand the necessary elements of court rules and structure, and to feel comfortable enough in that setting to testify truthfully and fully about what they have witnessed or experienced.

Because more and more children are being asked to testify in criminal court proceedings due to increased prosecution of child abuse cases, a book of this sort fills a very urgent need. It provides concrete suggestions to individuals preparing children to testify in court—regarding what they need to do before ever meeting with the child witness, how to include the family in the process, and specific suggestions about what (and what not) to do in court preparation. A chapter by a seasoned prosecutor, Thomas Fallon, addresses preparation issues for prosecutors, making this book the perfect primer for court preparation of children.

Linda Marinaccio Pucci, PhD
Private Practice—Maryville, Tennessee

Acknowledgments

I am deeply indebted to many people who graciously assisted with the formation of this book. Your reading, commenting, editing, and frequent words of encouragement made this project happen. Each of you made such important and significant contributions in many ways.

Liz Ghilardi, MSW, and Linda Doro, MA, I am eternally grateful for your willingness to help from the very beginning of this project.

I wish to thank the following people, whose comments and insights were deeply appreciated: Sheri Berkani, JD; Sandra J. Bertelle, MA; Kelly Birschbach, JD; Professor Jon Conte; Lt. Lee J. Copen, MA; Geoff Dowse, JD; Thomas J. Fallon, JD; Mary Hart, JD; Brian K. Holmgren, JD; District Attorney Robert J. Jambois; Debra Johansen, PhD; Deputy District Attorney Susan Karaskiewicz; Honorable Barbara A. Kluka; Honorable Mary Kay Wagner Malloy; Honorable Michael S. Fisher; Sandor Marianyi, BS; Anna C. Salter, PhD; Paul Stern, JD; Victor Veith, JD; and K. Richard Wells, JD.

A special thank you goes to the incredibly helpful, talented, and knowledgeable staff at the American Prosecutors Research Institute, National Center for the Prosecution of Child Abuse in Alexandria, Virginia.

To my dear friend, Linda M. Pucci, PhD, for her constant encouragement, patience, and kindness. This book would never have been completed without her support.

To former District Attorney, Robert D. Zapf, I am deeply grateful for your unfailing encouragement and continued support to learn about child victim/child witness issues.

Reverend Daniel P. and Marjorie Bergeland from Duluth, Minnesota, have a very special place in my heart. You taught me the most about caring, loving, respecting, and helping others. You are magnificent role models for all humanity. This book is dedicated to you as my way of saying thank you for all that you have done for me and so many other people.

Educator Information: Building a Foundation

The professional who will educate a child witness about the court system will need to begin by building an informational foundation.

Topics discussed in this chapter are as follows:

A. Introduction information for court educators
B. The need for a court educator
  1. Suggested court education and preparation components
  2. Court schools
  3. A critical link
  4. Who could be a court educator?
C. Possible functions of a court educator
  1. Teach the "rules and language of court" to a child and the parent
  2. Serve as a resource or "friend of the court"
  3. Identify, discuss, and attempt to remedy common court-related worries or fears
  4. Engaging and working with the parent
    a. Some common worries or fears of parents
  5. Serve as a liaison between the child, parents, lawyers, and therapist, as needed
  6. Serve as a referral resource for the child witness and the family for intervention and other mental health services
  7. Serve as a support person for the child witness
D. Common problems encountered and learning the basic rules of court
  1. Coaching a witness—What it is and how to avoid being accused of it
  2. What to say to parents about their child's bringing up the subject
  3. The disclosure process for a child witnessd (delayed and/or disclosure to someone other than parent)
  4. Difficult familial problems when a defendant is known and loved
E. Suggested tools and supplies
  1. Making a representational doll

Introduction Information for Court Educators

Every year, thousands of cases of child abuse involving young witnesses are referred to the court system. The number of these referrals has increased dramatically in the past decade, and it is likely to continue to rise in the years to come. Despite a continuing media backlash against the prosecution of these cases and the reliability of child witnesses, children are testifying in court proceedings in ever-increasing numbers.

Crime, violence, divorce, accidents, and disputes in many forms occur everywhere in the world. Children are frequently direct victims of crime or witnesses to these events. Civilized society attempts to resolve conflict, disputes, or criminal conduct in courts of law. Courts are to be open and available to all.

Historically, children have been denied the right to be witnesses in court because they were thought to be incompetent or not credible due to their age and developmental limitations. Children were unrealistically expected to behave and respond in court on an adult level—something they are simply incapable of doing.

Although statutory changes in the rules regarding children's competency have removed some of these barriers, new challenges to children's testimony through taint hearings and suggestibility challenges, as well as restrictions on expert testimony explaining children's responses to their victimization, lurk on the horizon.

Children who do testify continue to experience unrealistic, adultlike expectations about their performance as witnesses by judges, jurors, and attorneys. When children understandably fail to satisfy this expectation because of their developmental limitations or the traumatic impact of their victimization, the response is generally one that accords their testimony less believability. Children should not be discriminated against, nor otherwise prevented from gaining access to our courts, simply because they are children.

This book is designed to serve as a foundation for people who find themselves dealing with anxious parents and child witnesses. Lawyers, victim/witness specialists, CASAs (Court Appointed Special Advocates), social workers, law enforcement officers, therapists, and community child advocates are among the professionals who may find themselves in this role.

A great deal of attention on preparation of parents and child witnesses for criminal court hearings is discussed in this book. Concentration on the criminal justice system was done deliberately because children are most likely to be called to testify in a criminal or delinquency court proceeding. These hearings frequently involve allegations where children are themselves victims of physical or sexual abuse or neglect, or have witnessed other forms of family violence including abuse of siblings, domestic violence, and homicide.

Criminal court hearings are usually the most challenging, demanding, confusing, and difficult environments for any witness. Issues involving the constitutional and statutory protections for the accused are at their peak in criminal proceedings and are likely to have a greater impact on the child witness and his or her family. If a child witness is properly prepared to enter and cope with the rigors of the criminal justice system, he or she should be able to manage the less demanding or less restrictive environments of family, juvenile, or civil court. The information and practical suggestions offered herein are easily applied to these other venues.

Because of the importance of understanding the complexities and demands of the criminal court venue, I have asked a highly respected prosecutor, Thomas Fallon, to write a chapter that broadly explains this process. Thomas shares both his extensive knowledge and his practical experience in explaining the role of prosecutors and the issues they face with child witnesses, as well as how prosecutors and court educators need to work together as a team to make the system work for children.

This book is an introduction to educating and preparing children and their parents about the court system. Included in this book are several infrequently discussed topics or issues that court educators and lawyers should be made aware of, such as behaviors to watch for in a courtroom, the documentation and reporting of violations of court orders, safety/security issues and plans, and common worries of child witnesses and their families. These issues, although not typically considered part of a traditional education/preparation process or program, warrant discussion because they can have a direct impact on the welfare and well-being of witnesses and their families.

Memory, trauma and memory, suggestibility of children, true versus false allegations, and proper forensic interviewing techniques are important topics that are *not* addressed in this book. These are significant issues that are too complex to be addressed in this primer book. There are several excellent books available that do address these issues in great detail. Anyone working with child victims or witnesses should be familiar with the current literature on this subject matter.

Children have limitations as witnesses in court, and steps must be taken to address specific deficits. However, children can be competent and accurate witnesses in court when appropriate preparation has taken place. Testifying in court is a potentially stressful experience for any witness, even more so for children who have been victimized. But participation in the court process, and having their voices heard, can also be a positive and healing experience for children. Appropriate preparation and education of children and their families can enable this participation and reduce the likelihood that stress will be damaging.

Our children deserve to be heard and treated with all of the respect, dignity, and sensitivity afforded adults. When we reflect these ideals in our preparation of children as witnesses, we facilitate the search for truth that the law demands.

The Need for a Court Educator

Many jurisdictions fail to provide a systemic connection within the criminal justice system for child witnesses and their families. There may be no clearly defined job duty that explains, in a clear manner, who should educate a child and his or her family about the complex criminal justice process, or how to address the concerns that parents and witnesses may have. This book suggests that the role of a "court educator" could serve as a vital link between child witnesses, their parents, lawyers, and other aspects of the criminal justice system.

Going to court can be a difficult experience for anyone, but this is especially true when the victim or witness is a child. One of the goals of preparation and education is to minimize the likelihood that the child will suffer negative court-related consequences (Lipovsky & Stern, 1997).

In some jurisdictions, a court educator may be the person who greets a child before going to court, gives the child a basic overview of the court process, takes the child on a courtroom tour, and is present as a supporter in the courtroom when the child testifies. This description may depict how some jurisdictions conduct their education and/or preparation duties. The listed functions, although important, fail to address some important issues and/or difficulties about which parents and child witnesses may worry. Not addressing the worries or fears of parents and child witnesses could have a negative impact on their overall ability and willingness to cooperate with the legal system.

The task of court education *and* preparation may be left to a prosecutor who may be overworked or may just choose not to devote the time needed to adequately talk with parents and their children about their concerns or problems. In some cases, child witnesses meet their lawyer for the first time just minutes before they are summoned to testify at a hearing, and they are not afforded the courtesy of learning what is going to take place or what will be expected of them.

In some jurisdictions, a social worker or law enforcement officer may try to explain what going to court will be like to a child and his or her parents during an investigation, or even in a hallway while the child is waiting to testify at a court hearing. In other locations, a therapist or school counselor may try to take on this task if it appears that a child client is going to court and no preparation process has been implemented.

Researchers are discovering that the educational foundation is a vital aspect to reducing stress and trauma for witnesses. As Lipovsky (1994) states, "Research findings suggest that approaches to improving children's experiences in the courtroom should focus on (a) interventions directed toward the child and family and (b) those that modify components of the court process itself" (p. 249).

Although the reviewed studies indicate that many children and their parents find the court process emotionally upsetting, they also reveal that court need not be a *traumatic* experience with long-term psychological sequelae.

Education focused specifically on the legal system was a significant component of the court preparation intervention described by Sas, Hurley, Austin, and Wolfe (1991). Education for children addressed court-related language, courtroom etiquette, rules for giving evidence, roles of people in court, and different possible outcomes of the court process. In addition, a model courtroom and judge's gown were used in role-play situations to teach children about court procedures.

SUGGESTED COURT EDUCATION AND PREPARATION COMPONENTS

- *Education:* This should include providing children with a thorough understanding of the legal system and what will be expected of them.
- *Stress management procedures:* This should include such techniques as deep breathing, focus points, or learning how to relax muscles when becoming upset.
- *Improving parental attitudes about court:* This includes identifying and addressing the worries and concerns that many parents have when their child is expected to become a witness in a court case.

Parents who are worried about their child's emotional well-being or the overall safety of their family (due to a child's disclosure or witnessing of an event) could become uncooperative or hostile. When a parent is uncooperative with the law or legal authorities, it is likely that his or her child will become similarly uncooperative. For this reason, it is important to identify and address as many concerns that a parent may have as soon as possible.

If early interventions on behalf of child victims are sensitive and well-managed, families may be less threatened by the system and more cooperative with the case investigation and prosecution. Research has consistently found that parental (and especially maternal) support can be invaluable to the child's emotional well-being (Whitcomb, 1993). Negative parental attitudes toward the criminal justice system have a direct impact upon children's improvement (Goodman et al., 1992).

COURT SCHOOLS

In some large communities, there are enough child witnesses to support structured group programs, often called "court schools." In addition to thorough education programs, including stress management techniques and courtroom tours, these formal programs provide a wealth of related materials to the child witness and his or her parents.[1]

A CRITICAL LINK

A professional court educator, working within the criminal justice system, can take the time necessary to serve as a significant critical link between the child; his or her family; and the lawyers, court system, law enforcement representative, and other community intervention agencies. A full-time professional could serve in this capacity, or there could be other people specifically trained to fulfill this role on an as-needed basis.

WHO COULD BE A COURT EDUCATOR?

Court educators could be lawyers, victim/witness professionals, or trained volunteers interested in assisting a child who is going to court. Most nonlawyer court educators will likely be victim/witness program professionals, Court Appointed Special Advocates (CASAs), child advocacy center staff (CAC), or other specifically trained court advocates. Other potential court educators could include social workers, law enforcement officers, or mental health professionals.

Possible Functions of a Court Educator

Listed below are some of the possible functions of a court educator and some of the more common issues or problems that a court educator is likely to encounter. There is a brief discussion about why a particular function is suggested, as well as what may help to perform that task.

Some functions of a court educator include the following:

1. *Teach the rules and language of court to a child and the parent.* Children
   and their parents should be informed about what will be expected
   of them. Listed below is a sample of a few topics that could be routinely discussed with a child witness. More discussion on this topic
   takes place in Chapters 2 and 3 of this book.

   A few examples of some basic rules of court:

   - Always tell the truth.
   - Don't guess at answers. (If you don't know an answer, say so. It
     is okay to not know everything.)
   - It is okay to ask for a break or time out. (The child needs to
     know how to indicate such a need, and to whom the request is
     made.)
   - People are expected to behave in court. Talk about what a judge
     is likely to do if someone misbehaves in court.

   A few examples of court-related language:

   - Explain common terms that a child is likely to hear in a court-
     room (i.e., "objection," "sustained," "overruled," "testimony,"
     "hearing").
   - A child will likely hear words or phrases he or she won't under-
     stand. The child will need to learn how to say he or she does not
     understand a question or a word used. The lawyers and judge
     should be made aware of any word recognition difficulties.

   An example of a word could cause a problem in court:

   Q: Could you *describe* what he was wearing?

   A: Huh?

   Q: Could you *describe* for the court what he was wearing?

   A: I don't know . . . I don't . . . uhh . . . what is that word?

   Q: Let me ask you the question another way. What did he
   have on?

   A: Jeans and his motorcycle shirt.

   Q: Thank you. I'm glad you let me know that I needed to use
   different words.

   A: That's okay.

2. *Serve as a resource for lawyers or as a "friend of the court" regarding the following:*[2]

- The child's ability to understand the court process
- The child's ability to testify in court
- The need to make modifications to the physical layout of the courtroom (e.g., a lower witness table and/or chair)
- The utilization of closed circuit television or videotaped testimony
- Language modifications when in court
- Length of the child's attention span and opportune hours of the day for optimal communication exchange
- The child's ability to be qualified as a witness

    A court educator could be in a position to attend to the typical concerns most lawyers have of child witnesses. A court educator may be able to provide advice concerning a particular child's ability to understand proceedings or the ability of a child witness to cope with the rigors of a court experience, or the educator may suggest techniques that could assist a child witness to testify more accurately in court.

    Examples of some typical concerns that lawyers have about child witnesses:

- Does this child have any physical, emotional, or other impairment requiring special attention? If yes, inform the lawyer what the difficulty is, and what remedies or approaches may be necessary to aid the witness (pre-trial motion considerations).
- Is this child so fearful of a defendant that the child may have difficulty recalling facts or testifying accurately? The educator may need to suggest potential remedies to the lawyer that may assist a witness, such as the use of trauma dolls (discussed in Chapter 5), or physical modification of a courtroom, videotaped deposition, or closed-circuit TV.
- Will this child witness understand typical words used in court or complicated questions about time, distance, or relationships, etc.?
- Will the witness be able to be qualified as a witness? Will the child be able to take an oath or affirmation?
- Will this child be able to correct mistakes made by an adult?
- What time of day will this witness be most alert?

3. *Identify, discuss, and attempt to remedy common court-related worries or fears a child witness has.*

Examples of typical concerns or worries of child witnessses:

- *Fear of seeing the defendant in the courtroom.* Identifying and talking about common worries or fears that a child witness has, and relaying that information to the appropriate lawyer, is an essential and critical function of a court educator. One of the greatest sources of perceived stress for the child eyewitness is the fear of seeing the accused during testimony (Chambers, 1995).
  - There are at least two studies concerning actual child witnesses that indicate that facing the defendant is especially intimidating to children. For most of these children, facing the defendant was the most negative and frightening aspect of testifying. In fact, fear of the defendant was related to children being less able to answer the prosecutor's questions in court and children expressing postprosecution dissatisfaction with the legal system (Tobey, Goodman, Batterman-Faunce, Orcutt, & Sachsenmaier, 1995). Working with children who are very fearful about seeing a defendant in court is discussed in Chapter 5.
- *"What will happen if he (the defendant) gets mad and yells at me in court?"* Children need to know how a particular judge is likely to respond to such outbursts. Many judges will warn or remove people who engage in disruptive and frightening conduct. Other judges may be more tolerant and permit some disruptive behavior before taking action. To answer this question, the court educator may need to know about the demeanor and temperament of individual judges. Prosecutors, lawyers, court clerks, or bailiffs who work regularly with a particular judge may be appropriate people with whom to talk about this issue.
- *Not being believed and fear of harsh questioning.* Commonly expressed fears or worries are about not being believed and enduring a harsh questioning experience in the courtroom (Lipovsky, 1994).
  - The criminal justice system was purposely designed to be adversarial. Divorce court, by nature and circumstance, is

also likely to be an antagonistic experience for a witness. In an adversarial process, people think that one side or the other is generally wrong and the other one right. Witnesses for opposing sides in a court case sometimes view themselves and the lawyers as enemies, competitors, or opponents. The adversarial process is difficult and confusing for many children to comprehend. Children are simply too young to understand the legal philosophy about finding "the truth" in the frequently disagreeable environment of confrontation and cross-examination.

◆ Adult or child witnesses who experience the confrontational aspect of being asked questions have a hard time not taking attacks or challenges to what they say personally. To children, the court experience is very personal. Research has demonstrated that elements of the child's experience within the legal system are associated with measured levels of distress. Although testimony, in and of itself, does not appear to be associated with negative emotional consequences, multiple testimonies and the harshness of the direct and cross-examination experiences are predictive of children's distress (Lipovsky, 1994).

◆ Helping child witnesses cope with the adversarial nature of a court hearing and significantly lessen the negative impact of such an encounter could be major functions of the court educator.

4. *Engaging and working with the parent.* The parent(s) is probably the most important factor in determining how well a child will cope with what happened. Even so, the parents are the most forgotten or ignored part of a case. Most parents will be willing and eager to help. Parents tend to become involved in cases no matter how much an investigator or prosecutor may ask them not to. Parents will do whatever they deem necessary to ensure the welfare and well-being of their child. To ensure that parents do not harm a case, it is important to talk with them about the issues involved and to discuss openly their worries or concerns.

Isolating or excluding parents from the court education and preparation process is not helpful for the child, and it can prove to be a big mistake. The court educator may be in an excellent position to spend time with parents—to listen to them; educate them; and gain their trust, respect, and cooperation.

Taking care of the parents of a child witness is as psychologically important as taking care of the child witness. Parents should be referred for treatment and intervention services as readily as the child victim or witness.

Some common worries or fears expressed by parents:

- ◆ *"I think I'm losing my mind! How could this happen to my child? I am so mad I could kill!"* Parents whose children have been exposed to a bad experience frequently express feelings of rage, guilt, fear, blame, or confusion. These feelings should not be dismissed or minimized. Spend time talking with the parents before approaching their child. Listen to the worries of the parents and try to address their concerns as quickly as possible.

- ◆ *"I have seen on TV what happens to witnesses in court. I don't want my child damaged or scarred for life, or ripped to shreds by some slick lawyer!"* Parents are likely to express feelings of great reluctance and anxiety about their child giving evidence in a courtroom. Some of this anxiety can be alleviated with proper education about what will likely happen or not happen in the courtroom.

  - ◆ Consider sharing with the parents the results of some research studies about the emotional effects that court has had on children. Some studies indicate that with proper care, the court experience need not be a negative one (Whitcomb, 1992a). Children can and do testify without suffering significant emotional trauma (Lipovsky & Stern, 1997).

  - ◆ Any inappropriate parental response should be addressed quickly and gently by the professional. Negative, blaming, or inappropriate responses by a parent sometimes can do as much damage to a child witness as the witnessed or experienced activity or crime. Many parents are so overwhelmed with their own feelings of guilt, blame, or denial that it is very difficult for them not to project these feelings onto their children (MacFarlane, 1986). Encourage parents to ask questions. Answering questions is a good way to share information. The more information parents have about the court process, the more likely it is that they will be tolerant and understanding about what is going on.

- ◆ The court educator could be in a position to share the parental concerns or worries with the case lawyer. This information exchange could help develop a bond of trust between the parent, child witness, court educator, and lawyer.

◆ *"What if my child is too scared to see the defendant?"* This is a common worry for both the child witness and the parents. As discussed earlier, when this issue is raised by the child, the court educator should inform the child (and the parents) about what a particular judge is likely to tolerate with respect to any disruptive or unusual behavior by the defendant.

- ◆ In addition to discussing a child's fear of seeing a defendant in the courtroom, or how a child will be treated by the lawyers, talk with the parents about their own nervousness or fears.

- ◆ Parents who are not familiar with the court process may have many worries because of misconceptions or other wrong information. It is not unusual to discover that parents are more anxious about court than their child. Children will look to their parents to determine how they should interpret a situation. Children who were previously fine may easily pick up on a parent's anxiety response about court and become worried, fearful, anxious, or even physically sick.

- ◆ Parents are a critical aspect of working with a child. If you do not have the support of the parents in a case, you will likely not have the cooperation of a child witness. For this reason, court educators and lawyers *must* include the parents in any education or preparation work.

◆ *"How long will this case drag on?"* (*Multiple adjournments or postponements*). Often, and particularly with cases involving child witnesses, it is in the defendant's interest to prolong proceedings, wagering on the child's failing memory and desire to want to forget and move on. But the justice system does not forget, and although the court may allow numerous continuances, the child remains on call.

- Continuances can sometimes be beneficial for the prosecution, such as when the child is recanting. But some critics believe that more often, the effect of repeated continuances and delays is devastating, both to child victims and to the quality of their testimony (Whitcomb, 1992c). After working with thousands of crime victims and witnesses, experience has shown that case adjournment is one of the primary reasons that they become disgusted, frustrated, less cooperative, or even hostile toward the criminal justice system. Victims and witnesses want their court cases to be resolved as quickly as possible.

- When witnesses are subpoenaed to appear at court, they usually need to make personal arrangements to accommodate the order to appear. This may mean taking time off from school or work, and arranging transportation or child care, in addition to the stress from anticipation about what the experience will be like. Some witnesses become so stressed by the anticipation of testifying that they become physically ill.

- Because of the negative reactions that witnesses have from adjournments, it is recommended that the court educator specifically spend time preparing the witness and his or her parents for the likelihood that delays will occur. People who are not made aware of the common adjournment problem may believe that they are being treated unfairly or are being personally discriminated against.

- It is not unusual for previously cooperative parents and witnesses to become uncooperative or even hostile following unanticipated or multiple case adjournments. This is especially true if the witness went to trouble coordinating his or her personal schedule to accommodate being in court. The more times a witness is put through the adjournment process, the more upset and uncooperative he or she will become.

- Witnesses and family members should be given realistic timetables from which they can anticipate or plan their lives. Victims and witnesses who had been alerted to the adjournment problem at the beginning of their contact with the criminal justice system tended to be less anguished by the adjournment notices than were those who were not so prepared. Be prepared to explain the reasons for any case delay, and do so in a manner that is clear to the witnessses. Fortunately, many states are working on statutory reforms that will expedite the handling of cases involving child witnesses.

5. *Serve as a liaison between the child, parents, lawyers, and therapist, as needed.* During the course of litigating a case, a court educator could serve as a person to whom the child and parents can go whenever they have particular questions, concerns, or problems. The criminal justice system is made up of many different professionals. The roles and functions of the many system professionals a family can encounter can be quite confusing. Parents and children are frequently overwhelmed by the numbers of different people they meet during a court process. Parents often wonder about whom to contact when they have concerns. A court educator could serve as one clearly identified person with whom the child or parent can turn to for advice, assistance, or referral.

When witnesses or parents have questions or concerns, they generally expect a speedy return call. A court educator is likely to be better able to respond more quickly to inquiries than a case lawyer. Lawyers are often in court all day, and when they return to their offices, they are not likely to spend the needed amount of time talking with individual witnesses or parents about their problems or worries. Performing this liaison function can be comforting to confused and worried witnesses or parents, and it can serve as a much needed conduit of information to the case lawyer, law enforcement officer, social worker, therapist, or other appropriate professionals within the system.

When inquiries or comments about worries, fears, or needs are discovered, the court educator could be in a unique position to assist with making connections to secure proper services or interventions in a timely manner. Children and families deserve the best attention that our legal system can provide. Giving parents and witnesses access to someone identified within the legal system who will respond promptly to questions or concerns, and being

able to attend appropriately to their needs, will greatly enhance the
confidence level of witnesses in our legal system.

6. *Serve as a referral resource for the child witness and the family for intervention or other mental health services.* Court educators could serve
   as a resource for parents and child witnesses by having up-to-date
   community mental health or intervention program information
   readily available for distribution and referral.

7. *Serve as a support person for the child witness.* A court educator could
   be with a child witness in a courtroom when he or she is called
   upon to testify. The court educator could be with the child witness
   before a hearing, during testimony, and following the hearing.

Common Problems Encountered and Learning the Basic Rules of Court

There are a number of common problems likely to be encountered by
court educators and lawyers during the pendency of a court case. The
following are a few of the more common difficulties.

The following are some common issues of legal or psychological
importance:

- Coaching a witness—what it is, and how to avoid being accused
  of it
- Proper and improper activities to discuss with parents
- The disclosure process for a child witness (i.e., delayed disclosure
  or disclosure to someone other than the parent)
- Difficult familial problems when a defendant is known and loved

COACHING A WITNESS—WHAT IT IS AND HOW TO AVOID BEING ACCUSED OF IT

"Coaching a witness" occurs when someone helps to determine answers to questions. Naive, ill-informed, but well-intentioned people
sometimes feel compelled to do a practice session with a child witness
involving his or her actual testimony. Refrain completely from asking
questions of a witness about the pending case. *Do not rehearse testimony!*

Anyone working with a child who is going to go to court to testify
must learn the rules about coaching a witness. The rule is, *don't discuss*

the facts of a case unless you are trained to do so, or are a lawyer assigned to work on this particular case. Rehearsed testimony could be disqualified and never heard by a jury.

Conduct that may appear to be coaching can include the following:

- *A nonlawyer asking a witness specific case questions so that the listener will know what the child is going to say in court.* Although there is no real tampering going on when only *listening* to an answer, the charge of coaching a witness could be raised. This is not to be confused with the duty of a lawyer to talk with potential witnesses in this regard. Lawyers have a legal duty to meet with and talk with witnesses about what they saw, heard, or had happen to them.

- *A parent or someone else discussing what happened with a child witness, when the child is not the person to bring up the subject.* It is not unusual for parents or other adults in a child's life to be upset about what a child has disclosed, and they may feel compelled to talk about it with the child. Some adults say, "I needed to hear it from her myself." Sometimes, this compulsion happens again and again with the same or different people. This type of behavior *could* be viewed by some as tampering with, rehearsing, or coaching a witness, as the following example illustrates.

  In a Florida case, a 5-year-old witness conceded that his mother, the alleged victim of a crime, had told him "what to say." The trial court pursued the possibility that the child's memory had become tainted. The following exchange occurred between the court and the child's mother:

  Q: Did you talk to him about what took place at the deposition?

  A: Well, my husband talked to him then.

  Q: And today before you came in here and when he came in, you refreshed his memory?

  A: Refresh his memory, I did.

  Q: As to what you did and you reminded him of all the different facts to be sure he remembered them all?

  A: Not everything, I just told him to get up here and tell the truth, what he knew, and talk loud.

  Q: Did you also remind him of some of the facts, certain things, you refreshed his memory as to what had taken place?

A: Of what happened, yes, I did.

> The trial judge did not find this above activity to be problematic and the trial continued. The defendant was convicted and the case was appealed. In *Davis v. State* (Fla. Appeal. 1977), the Florida Court of Appeal subsequently reversed the trial court, substituting its finding that the child was "incompetent" to testify, after noting that the record of the trial proceedings was "permeated with instances of undue influence over [the child] by his parents" (McGough, 1994, p. 96).

Parents should be advised to *not discuss* what the child is going to say in court. Reassure the parents that the lawyer will discuss the child's testimony at the proper time and in a proper manner.

There will be times, however, when the child needs to talk with a parent or trusted person about what happened. Although parents are to be cautioned not to bring up the topic with the child, they should also be asked to not stop their child from talking about it if it is the child who needs to do so. Parents will need to know that children may choose to talk about it and may select an inconvenient or unexpected moment to do so.

It is important for parents to do their best to control exhibiting any strong feelings or reactions to what their child is saying. Children have an exquisite ability to read faces—especially those of people whom they love. When children talk about what happened, it is important that adults refrain from demonstrations of shock, anger, or hurt. These reactions can easily be misinterpreted by the child as feelings about them, rather than about the information being revealed.

WHAT TO SAY TO PARENTS ABOUT THEIR CHILD'S BRINGING UP THE SUBJECT

When parents ask what they should do when the child brings up facts about the crime, the court educator could consider giving the following advice:

- Listen to the child.
- Refrain from asking the child questions. Gently encourage the child to talk as much as he or she needs.

- Control emotions or expressions of shock, horror, disgust, or anger (hugs and other physical comforting, however, may be very much needed by the child and would be very appropriate).

Proper and Improper Activities for Parents

It may be helpful for court educators to consider preparing a written list of activities for parents that could help or hurt their case.

Parents *should* do the following:

- Help the child complete his or her court education workbook.
- Help the child understand the legal words listed in the workbook.
- Inform the court educator about how the concept of "telling the truth" or "telling a lie" is addressed in their home. Are the words *truth* or *lie* used in their home? What words are used in their home to describe what is the truth and what is a lie? (Some parents teach their children about "fibs," and don't use the word "lie" in their home.)
- Explain to the educator and lawyer what would typically happen in their home if someone did something wrong. What are typical modes of discipline in their home?
- Relay expressed worries, fears, or questions to the court educator and lawyer.
- Explain to the court educator any religious, personal, or cultural difficulties this family may have with any aspect of a traditional court process.
- Inform the court educator and lawyer when their child's best and worst times of the day are. When does the child take a nap? When is the child most alert and attentive?
- Display a confident and positive attitude about going to court to the child.

Parents *should not* do the following:

- Rehearse or practice testimony.
- Force a child to talk about what happened when the child does not initiate the conversation.

- Prevent the child from discussing what happened when the child wants or needs to do so.
- Conduct an independent investigation (such as traveling with the child to the scene of a crime, or independently talking with witnesses, or surveilling a defendant).
- Express worries, fears, or negative feelings about the case or court in front of, or within hearing distance of, the child.

THE DISCLOSURE PROCESS FOR A CHILD WITNESS (DELAYED DISCLOSURE OR DISCLOSURE TO SOMEONE OTHER THAN THE PARENT)

Some children tell about experiencing or witnessing a criminal event right away. Some children tell their parent(s) first. Other children don't tell about hearing, seeing, or having something happen to them right away. They may disclose this information to someone other than their parents first.

Parents typically report feeling hurt, angry, or betrayed when they discover that their child failed to tell them first about a criminal or troubling event or experience. They express feelings of shock, disappointment, anger, and even disbelief when they discover their child did not tell them first about something being wrong or troublesome. If a child discloses victimization or witnessing an event to someone other than the parent, or delays telling a parent about a situation, it is extremely important that the common nature of this behavior be explained to the parent as soon as possible.

For children who have been victimized by abuse, the act of disclosing abuse is a difficult decision to make. It has been suggested that the majority of children never disclose until adulthood, if at all (Lamb & Edgar-Smith, 1994). As a matter of fact, some studies indicate that most ongoing sexual abuse is *never* disclosed, at least not outside the immediate family (Summit, 1983).

Why do people delay or fail to disclose being victimized or witnessing a crime? People who delay or fail to report experiencing or witnessing a bad event report that the primary reason they stayed silent was due to fear.

Listed below are some of the more commonly stated reasons or fears of victims and why they failed to disclose their victimization or delayed reporting:

- Fear of hurting their parents, if the victim is a child, or fear of hurting a nonoffending parent, if the other parent is the perpetrator
- Fear of retaliation or harm from an offender or his or her family (either in the form of direct personal harm or harm to family, pets, or property)
- Fear of being blamed for causing trouble (for the offender, or in the home, neighborhood, school, or community)
- Fear of losing the love or approval of people about whom the witness cares
- Fear that he or she may have done something wrong and would be in trouble, too
- Fear of feeling overwhelming shame or guilt
- Fear of not being believed or listened to

It is important for parents to know that their child needs their love, support, and understanding. Who their child disclosed to first is really not all that important. What is important, however, is that the child told someone.

DIFFICULT FAMILIAL PROBLEMS WHEN A DEFENDANT IS KNOWN AND LOVED

If a child is a victim of a crime in which the perpetrator was not previously known, family support is usually quite strong. There will be times, however, when cases involving strangers will present reluctant parents. The reasons given for this reluctance are usually the parents' desire to protect their child from a harsh court experience, fears about retaliation, and long court delays.

In cases in which the child and perpetrator are related by blood or marriage, or in which the perpetrator is a close friend of the family, a clash may occur, causing previously friendly relationships to become bitter and even hostile. A hostile environment is very difficult for anyone to live in, but it is especially difficult for a child because children cannot move away from the problematic environment or understand why there would be conflict, bitterness, or hostility from people who were previously loving, caring, and nurturing toward him or her.

Some dangerous symptoms or behaviors found in children who are trying to survive in some nonsupportive or hostile environments are depression, withdrawal, suicide attempts, running away, eating and sleep disturbances, and recantation (Sorenson & Snow, 1991). For these reasons, court educators need to be aware of these family dynamics in order to try to help parents lessen the negative impact on their child before problems become destructive, solidified, and unmanageable.

Children in highly charged or stressful family situations may refuse to answer questions about the event at all. Some children have revealed that they thought their telling was the reason why their family became "mad" or "mean." Some children may recant what they had previously reported as a way to get the family to stop fighting. The pressure a child experiences in these situations is enormous and sometimes unbearable.

Adults need to learn how important it is to keep an open mind, not pick sides, and withhold judgment—at least until all of the facts are brought out in an appropriate environment. Try to get angry or upset family members of a child victim or witness into a neutral emotional place regarding the issue of who to believe. This challenging task may be achieved by spending some time in a warm and neutral educational setting with these adults.

Consider talking about general dynamics of typical cases, as well as the court process, such as how factual evidence will be revealed over a period of time, and the need to be patient with the court process. Following such meetings, some relatives may try very hard to not openly choose sides, and they may behave neutrally toward the child involved. Others may not be so inclined and will cling to their anger and outrage.

This information is valuable for court educators to know, because they can work with the child's parents to help find ways to insulate the child from contact with negative individuals.

Suggested Tools and Supplies

Court educators will need to have supplies and tools to begin the process of educating children and their parents about the court process. Listed below are some suggested standard court-related educational supplies to consider having available for use.

- *Hand puppets.* These might be useful when initially greeting or meeting with a child witness.
- *Drawing easel and paper.* Drawing pictures can be an effective means of engaging a child in a verbal discussion with the court educator or lawyer. Having paper on an easel will afford the court educator an opportunity to position him- or herself next to the child for communication purposes in a more comfortable manner. Easels typically come equipped with pads of white paper.
- *Crayons, washable magic markers, and regular and colored pencils.* An assortment of crayons, markers, pens, or pencils should be made available for a child to use when coloring or drawing.
- *Child scissors.* For safety concerns, scissors used by a child should be appropriate for his or her age and developmental level.
- *Sheets of white and colored paper.* Although many children will readily use the easel and paper, there may be occasions when they would prefer to draw at a table with a single sheet of paper, or will desire colored paper for their works of art.
- *A set of building blocks.* Building blocks are not only objects that provide children with enjoyment, but also tools that can easily be used to assess a child's ability to follow directions or understand certain words (i.e., please put one block *on top* of another, or please place the *yellow* block *next to* the green block).
- *A timer with a bell and a clock with a sweep second hand.* A bell timer will be used to set "work time" and "no work time" with a child witness. A clock with a sweep second hand will be used to help determine a child's ability to understand seconds and minutes.
- *Court-related coloring workbooks.* Court-related coloring workbooks are used to help explain typical court words and court people, as well as the physical furnishings the child will likely encounter.[3]

- *A miniature replica of a judge's robe.* A child-size replica of a judge's black robe can be worn by the child during educational and prepa-ration work. Wearing the robe helps to demystify that particular uniform.

- *A child-size gavel.* A child size gavel is a fun way to introduce the child to a standard piece of equipment that many children expect to find in a courtroom.

- *Model miniature courtroom or drawing of a courtroom.* Children need to see where things are located. Many children are unable to con-ceptualize by verbal descriptions how court will look. Gently in-troducing a child to the concept of court by way of a replica is usu-ally enjoyable, manageable, and not overwhelming. After a child has been introduced to a courtroom in this nonthreatening manner, an actual tour will be far less intimidating. Many stores have toy departments where toy chairs and tables may be purchased for the creation of a miniature courtroom model. A drawing, sketch, or cardboard box (designed to depict a courtroom) may be substi-tuted if a formal model miniature courtroom is unavailable in your area.

  Children should be shown where the judge, jury, court reporter, court clerk, lawyers, and witnesses are likely to be seated when he or she goes into the real courtroom. Explain how the courtroom model or drawing is different from or similar to the real courtroom that the child will be visiting. Tell the child some general informa-tion about the individual people he or she is likely to encounter in the real courtroom.

- *Glue, glitter, beads, sequins, feathers, ribbon, fabric (for use with next item)*

- *Cardboard or heavy construction paper, or small, unpainted wooden hu-man form dolls with which to make representational dolls.* A represen-tational doll depicts someone about whom the child loves or cares, but who cannot be in the courtroom when the child testifies. The doll could depict a parent, favorite teacher, aunt, uncle, or anyone whom the child likes. The child is permitted to take the doll to court in a pocket where it can be held or touched whenever the child feels the need to feel the missing loved one. When the child is done testi-fying, he or she can be given the representational doll to keep.

MAKING A REPRESENTATIONAL DOLL

Start with a 2-inch piece of wood or cardboard cutout in the shape of a simple human form. Use a penny or nickel to make the doll's head and draw in a body to fit the head on the paper. The child decorates or colors the doll any way he or she chooses.

- *Adhesive tape.* Adhesive tape is used to display works of art by the child and to make repairs to drawings.
- *Two toy telephones.* Some hesitant children will engage in conversation with the court educator when a toy telephone is used to "talk."
- *An assortment of standard children's books.* It is recommended that audio books be included in this assortment. (Books that have "sound" buttons that can be pushed to make noises are especially attractive to children.)
- *An assortment of stickers.* Colorful and fun stickers are placed on work done during the education process. All children, no matter how incomplete the work is, should receive a sticker.
- *Anatomical drawings.* Anatomical drawings that are blank may be needed by the lawyer during his or her discussions with a child witness and should be readily available for use.
- *Child-size chairs, table, and bean-bag chair.* An assortment of furniture sizes should be available in the education or preparation area to provide a child with a selection for his or her comfort.
- *Photograph album.* Children can be shown a photograph album that contains pictures of court personnel whom the child is likely to meet. The album is one method of introducing the topic of court to children. Most children readily enjoy looking at pictures, and the album serves as a nice introductory step for court education. Consider inserting the following photographs inside a court-people album:

  - ◆ Court educator

  - ◆ Lawyers (prosecutor, defense, guardian ad litem, etc.)

  - ◆ Victim/witness program staff

- ◆ Bailiff

- ◆ Court clerk

- ◆ Court reporter

- ◆ Court law enforcement personnel

- ◆ Social worker

- ◆ CASA or child advocate volunteers

- ◆ Judge (Some children are quite fearful or anxious about seeing or meeting the judge. Photographs of judges should be included in the album in two ways—in full black robe seated at the bench, and in regular street clothes not seated at the bench.

Pictures of all the actual courtrooms used in a community should be included in the album so that the child can see photographs of their real courtroom before the introductory courtroom tour.

Notes

1. Information about two such programs is listed here, although there are many such programs throughout the country: Children's Hospital and Health Care, Center for Child Protection, 8001 Forest Street, San Diego, CA 92123; The Philadelphia Court School Project, Office of the District Attorney, Philadelphia, PA.

2. See Wisconsin § 950.055(2)(c) and Washington § 7.69A.030(4)(5). Many states have or are working on enacting legislation that would enable a court educator to provide these functions.

3. Sage Publications publishes a children's educational work/coloring book titled *Getting Ready for Court: A Book for Children*. This workbook is available in either a criminal court or a civil court edition.

2

Preparing to Perform Duties and Functions

There are some difficult issues a court educator or lawyer will likely encounter when working with child witnesses and their families. The purpose of this chapter is to suggest some approaches that could help address some of the more frequently encountered difficulties or dilemmas. Each community will need to decide how it will respond to the many problems encountered. Another consideration for community professionals working with child witnesses is that of deciding who is in the best position to respond to these identified problems. This book suggests that there is a need to be prepared to respond to a variety of situations that occur on occasion.

Topics discussed in this chapter are as follows:

A. Assessing the case: To review or not review case facts?
B. The court educator as a potential witness
C. Safety and security issues:
    1. Out-of court safety and security issues
        a. The defendant's background
        b. Bail bond/court orders
        c. Threats, harassment, communication
    2. In-court safety and security issues
        a. The defendant's demeanor
        b. Control cuing
        c. Hostile courtroom spectators
        d. Preparing a standard safety plan
    3. Other basic safety tips

Assessing the Case: To Review or Not Review Case Facts?

If the primary function of a court educator is to give children a court-house tour and an overview of your court system, you may not need to be familiar with the underlying facts of the case. But if a court educator's function is to educate the child witness about court, answer questions posed by parents, be with the child in court for support purposes, and give advice to the lawyer or judge about a child's ability to cope with the criminal justice process, then the court educator may need to know what information the witness has revealed.

During the educational and acquaintance process with the child and his or her family, the court educator could receive information about the case from the witness that was not previously discussed with law enforcement, social services, or the lawyer. It is not unusual for victims, witnesses, or even parents to disclose additional information during the court education process.

Without prior knowledge of the case facts, a court educator will not know if information being revealed during the educational process is new, different, consistent, or inconsistent with prior statements. It is possible that some important piece of information could be ignored, mishandled, or not relayed to appropriate people. The possibility of additional case facts being disclosed to the court educator is quite possible if a warm and trusting relationship has developed between the child, his or her parents, and the court educator.

Being knowledgeable about the facts of a case does not mean that the court educator should discuss them. A court educator should listen to what a child is saying during the educational process, but not further investigate a crime or interrogate a witness. Any new or different information discovered by the court educator should be given to the case lawyer as soon as possible following the educational session.

The Court Educator Becoming a Potential Witness

What happens if the court educator becomes a witness due to additional information being disclosed during the educational process? The disclosure of additional information to a court educator could pose a problem if the professional is also expected to accompany the child witness to court as a supporter. It is not unusual for court educators to be subpoenaed by defense lawyers, whether or not a child has revealed information about a case. Don't panic or worry about being subpoenaed.

If a child discloses additional information to the court educator, a full report detailing the exact content and manner in which the disclosure came about must be prepared and given to the case lawyer immediately. If the lawyer thinks there is a possibility that the court educator may be needed as a witness in the future, or if the defense lawyer subpoenas the original court educator, do your best to locate another professional to serve as the in-court supporter as soon as possible. Enlist the aid of the child in the selection process of a new supporter, if you have more than one candidate in mind, and make arrangements for the witness and new "court friend" to meet. Try to select a substitute court friend who is unlikely to be subpoenaed during the case.

The court educator should try to appear calm and positive when talking with the child about also being subpoenaed. Children are usually comforted with the knowledge that someone they liked and trusted enough to reveal additional information to (the subpoenaed court educator) is also going to go to court to talk to the judge.

With advance notice of this substitution, and with some comfortable meetings between the original court educator, child, and new supporter, the transfer of support responsibility usually progresses quite smoothly.

Court educators should not get overly concerned about becoming a potential witness in a case. There are many positive aspects to being called as a witness in a case. The fear of becoming a potential witness should not stop a court educator from paying careful attention to what a child witness says during the educational or preparation process and reporting whatever information is revealed to the case lawyer.

Safety and Security Issues

Safety is going to be a common concern expressed by most people. Court educators, lawyers, and law enforcement officers need to work together to ensure that safety and security issues are identified and addressed promptly. Some form of safety assessment should be performed on every case by the law enforcement officer, court educator, and lawyer.

Everyone involved should have a thorough understanding of the potential problems and the impact they can have on the lives of witnesses. A security or safety assessment could begin when the court educator is reviewing the facts of a case in preparation for meeting a child witness. Try to determine the background and nature of a defendant, any revelations of threats, coercion, gang affiliations, and so on. This information is likely to be part of the law enforcement/prosecutor's case file. The lawyer needs to know this information to properly prepare a bond argument when the defendant appears in court (see the discussion of bail bonds).

Safety issues can generally be divided into two categories: out-of-court safety or security considerations and in-court safety or security considerations.

OUT-OF-COURT SAFETY OR SECURITY CONSIDERATIONS

What to seek out for information-gathering purposes:

1. The defendant's background
2. Bail bonds and court orders
   ◆ Violations of no-contact orders
3. Threats, harassment, communication
   ◆ Telephone threats
   ◆ Notes, letters, presents—usually unsigned
   ◆ Third-party communication

The Defendant's Background

What may be learned from someone's criminal background? If a defendant has a history of violence or witness intimidation, or has threatened/harassed prior victims or witnesses, it is likely that this could occur during the pendency of this case. Be concerned when past conduct demonstrates a disregard for court orders, rules, or authority figures, or if it contains elements of violent or threatening conduct. Most law enforcement officers will include a local background record check when investigating anyone for a crime.

The results of a local investigative background check will likely be included in any case file submitted to a prosecutor's office for a charging decision. In addition to a local record check, review what is commonly referred to as a "triple I" (III), which is an Interstate Identification Index. If someone has been arrested anywhere in the United States, this information should be available through the III database, which is accessible only through law enforcement agencies.

Not all cases will have security issues that become problematic, but nobody knows for sure which cases will have security difficulties and which ones will not. There are some clues, however, that should serve as a red flag on specific cases. Court educators and lawyers should automatically heighten concern for victim/witness safety if they note the following situations during the examination of a defendant's history or background:

- *Defendants arrested for or have had police contacts involving domestic violence or any form of violence.* Read the details about any previously reported incident of violence involving this same defendant. This information may be helpful if the pending case is related to family violence, or if the same people are involved once more. How someone has behaved in the past may give clues as to how that person may behave in the future.

- *Defendants who have been investigated or arrested for stalking, harassment, or injunction violations.* Read any reports regarding these charges or allegations. This information could provide some insight about how the defendant behaves and what conduct he or she may consider engaging in with the pending case.

- *Defendants who have violated prior court orders (i.e., having contact with witnesses when ordered to not do so).* Secure copies of any reports concerning this conduct. This demonstrates a disregard for rules and a disrespect for authorities. Such a person is unlikely to heed future warnings from law enforcement officers or judges to leave victims and witnesses in a new case alone.

- *Defendants with recorded incidents of "no-shows" for court hearings on other cases, or "no-shows" for probation/parole appointments.* This can be used by the lawyer to argue for a cash bond, because this person has demonstrated a willingness to not appear when expected for appointments or hearings.

- *Defendants with known violent gang affiliation and/or involvement.* It is not unusual for gang-affiliated defendants to arrange for harassment, intimidation, or threats to victims or witnesses. Safety plans must be made *in advance* of being needed to permit a quick and effective systemic response to reported problems.

The following is an example of what may be learned by reviewing historical data about a defendant:

> Emilio was arrested three separate times in the past. Following each arrest, key witnesses received a typed note, attached to a dead rose, in their mailbox. The note said, "Shut up or blow up." Witnesses who received these notes also reported attempted arson fires to their homes, severed telephone lines, and slashed tires on their vehicles. Following these events, the witnesses refused to testify in court, and Emilio was not convicted of his prior activities. What is the likelihood that witnesses in the current case will be intimidated or threatened? Quite high. Safety precautions and police surveillance should be strongly encouraged.

Bail Bonds and Court Orders

People accused of and charged with committing crimes will have a hearing in which charges are reviewed and a bond is set. The purpose of a bond is to ensure the appearance of a defendant at future court hearings. In addition to money being paid, many courts will attach additional conditions to that bond. These conditions are stated in open court, and the defendant must agree to follow them.

In criminal court cases, it is common for the court to issue release conditions that require a defendant to have no contact with specified victims or witnesses to the crime. In addition to a no-contact order, it may be common for courts to order other conditions, such as no consumption of alcoholic beverages or nonprescribed drugs (when they were a factor in a case), no violation of any laws while out of jail on bond, and so on. Violations of any court order should be reported, documented, and investigated. Violations of bond conditions may be viewed as contempt of court or prosecuted as bail jumping, a new, chargeable criminal act.

Violations of no-contact orders. Violations of no-contact orders in criminal cases are a common complaint. Court educators and lawyers will need to be prepared to respond promptly and properly to these allegations.

Victims of crime frequently report fears that a defendant will attempt to hurt or scare them when they are released from jail. Unfortunately, most violations of the no-contact rule seem to happen after the close of regular business hours at the courthouse, where court documents are kept.

One way to help witnessses and parents become prepared to handle this type of crime is to provide them with a valid copy of any no-contact order, as well as instructing them about reporting these serious violations. Without an appropriate document in the hands of a parent, any victim or witness (or parent) who calls a law enforcement agency to report a violation will likely receive the following response:

> "I'm sorry, ma'am. There is nothing I can do about what you just reported. I don't know what a judge has ordered in your case! Without some proof of what you are saying, we can't make an arrest. Call the prosecutor's office in the morning and report it to them."

If there is a specific no-contact order as a condition of a bond, provide each specified person (or his or her parents) with two copies of the court order. Generally, no-contact orders prohibit *any* form of contact, including direct contact, indirect contact through a third party, or communication by letter or telephone. The witness should carry one copy at all times, and the other copy should be kept in a safe place at his or her home or place of work.

If a defendant violates a no-contact order, the victim or witness will have immediate proof that such conduct is prohibited by a lawful court order. An investigating law enforcement officer will be able to verify quickly the validity of the order (especially if the documents are officially notarized by the Clerk of Court office in your jurisdiction). With proper documentation, a law enforcement officer can effect an immediate arrest, if deemed appropriate.

Prepare written instructions for parents, along with the two copies of certified bond orders, on official letterhead stationery. This letter, along with the official bond document, will help any responding law enforcement officer to verify the lawful order and to better understand the situation.

The instructions to parents should have the following information:

- In the heading, include the name of the prosecutor and his or her telephone number, the name of the court educator and his or her telephone number, and the defendant's name and court file number.
- Provide instructions on how to report a violation:
  - Call the local law enforcement agency number
  - List the name of the primary case detective
  - Tell the police officer all the details of a violation
  - Tell the police officer about any physical evidence, such as a recorded telephone message, letter, or package
  - Show the police officer a copy of the bond order

Threats, Harassment, Communication

Knowing in advance the answers to common questions will not only serve to expedite the assistance process but also provide some measure of comfort to the victim or witness because you were anticipating their needs.

Telephone threats. A very common method of delivering a threat to a witness is by telephone. The court educator must know how your community responds to these situations. Victims and/or parents are to report any contact that involves threats, harassment, or violations of court orders to law enforcement *immediately*. Most law enforcement agencies will want a victim to note the date, time, and specific content of any conversation.

Inform victims, witnesses, and family members to remove and preserve carefully any tape from a telephone answering machine that has recorded any message from a defendant if a responding law enforcement officer is unable or unwilling to retrieve the tape for evidence.

Defendants held in jail generally must make collect telephone calls from a cell block area. Accepted collect calls will be listed on a victim's telephone bill, which could serve as proof that the call was made on a specific date, time, and location. However, parents should be advised to not accept collect telephone calls and to be suspicious if they receive one. If a defendant is making calls from jail, it may be possible to restrict his or her access to a telephone if that privilege is being abused. The case lawyer may be able to talk with the appropriate jail supervisor about restricting telephone access by a particular defendant.

Parents should report suspicious hang-up calls to their local telephone authorities and give them permission to have a trace conducted on their telephone line. Hang-up calls should be documented by recording on a tablet the date and time of each occurrence.

The following are questions to which a court educator should have answers before meeting with victims or witnesses in any case:

1. How will law enforcement in my community respond to telephone threats?
2. What is the procedure to report this crime to a telephone company or law enforcement agency?
3. What procedures are to be followed when a telephone call must be recorded and/or traced?
4. Will the victim need to keep a logbook that documents the date, time, and substance of any unusual or threatening telephone call?
5. To whom should a victim or parent report a threat?
6. Will a report be filed with the police, or is the crime reported to the prosecutor first and then referred to the police?
7. What types of criminal charges, if any, may be brought for threatening telephone calls in your jurisdiction?
8. Is it permitted in your state to audiotape telephone calls with one-party consent, as proof or evidence that a crime happened, or is this considered illegal? Some states permit the taping of telephone calls with the consent of one party (usually the victim or parent). In other locations, this activity is considered illegal and cannot be suggested or implemented.

Notes, letters, and other presents. In addition to telephone calls, it is fairly common for victims or witnesses to receive letters in the mail or notes left on car windshields and other places from defendants or their supporters. If a victim or witness receives any communication that is thought to be from a defendant, they should call the law enforcement authorities immediately and *not* touch the document any more than absolutely necessary.

Sometimes, flowers, stuffed animals, knives, dead animals, and other "gifts" are mysteriously left on car windshields, porches, driveways, and so on. Although these items rarely yield fingerprints or source origination evidence, they should be properly reported, photographed by the police, and held as evidence.

Third-party messages. Some defendants believe that they are circumventing the direct no-contact order by asking a friend, relative, or other person to deliver a message to the victim or witness. These contacts, and the identity of the messenger, should be reported to law enforcement authorities immediately.

IN-COURT SAFETY AND SECURITY CONSIDERATIONS

What to look for in the defendant:

1. Demeanor/behavior
2. Control cuing or manipulation
3. Hostile spectators

The Defendant's Demeanor

Children frequently report being fearful or anxious about seeing the defendant in court. Some offenders will present themselves as sad and pathetic creatures. Some even cry in the courtroom. Some children will be terrified about seeing a defendant in a courtroom and will have great difficulty just entering the same room as this person.

Criminals have strong incentives to manipulate victims into recanting allegations or key witnesses into "forgetting" what they saw, or otherwise being uncooperative with the state (Veith, 1994).

Many criminals have the need to control their crime victims. In many cases, this control can, but need not, involve force or the threat of force. Sometimes, the manipulation comes in the form of expressions of great love or generous acts. Other times, the manipulation and control can be achieved by a look, gesture, or stare, which will be referred to as "control cuing."

Control Cuing

Some offenders resort to control cuing to terrify their victims into silence in a courtroom. Control cues are usually very subtle and seemingly innocuous expressions, gestures, smells (e.g., wearing a specific aftershave fragrance), or other nonverbal communications between the defendant and the victim/witness. Some offenders, when they commit their crimes, will deliberately incorporate certain signals, gestures, or even odors into their criminal behavioral repertoire.

Control cuing will likely happen in cases in which the offender knows his victim, and the criminal activity has been repetitive. The offender already knows how the victim responded to this cue in the past, and he will attempt to trigger a known response in the victim. Control cuing will take place in the courtroom and in front of everyone, but unless you know to look for it, it can be so innocent and subtle, it is missed by all except the intended target—the victim/witness.

When a control cue or signal has been used enough times between an offender and a victim, a victim need only see or hear the signal, and he or she knows what is about to occur. The special meaning behind these benign exchanges is usually known by the victim/witness and the offender. The victim/witness may not even be consciously aware that the cuing is going on. Control cuing can be difficult to detect unless professionals in the courtroom are attentive, observant, and know what cuing is.

Control cuing could be something as benign as the clicking of a pen, the placement of an object on a table (such as a coin or cigarette lighter), a special physical gesture or movement of the body, or the wearing of a particular fragrance.

One child fell silent in the courtroom when the offender put on a pair of sunglasses. The child immediately ceased talking and became motionless in the witness box. Nobody understood why the child, who was doing so well up to that point, was now frozen.

Later, the child was able to talk about what had happened. He revealed that the offender used to put on those same sunglasses just before inflicting physical pain on the child. The child said he was terrified by all the past memories of abuse that flooded back as soon as he saw the sunglasses in the courtroom. The child said he took this as a message that he was going to suffer great pain if he continued to talk in court. (Note: This defendant had the sunglasses in court because he told the transport officer that he needed the lenses for medical reasons during his trip from the jail facility to the courthouse.)

When reviewing case reports before meeting a victim or witness, look for the following information or indicators that malevolent control activities have likely taken place and a victim may be subjected to later control cuing in the courtroom:

- Reports of a victim being exposed to terror tactics (i.e., threats; actually witnessing the death or mutilation of people, pets, or effigies, such as a doll or toy)
- Evidence of physical torture used or threatened (i.e., reports of strangulation, beatings, starvation, burning, use of hot or cold water for immersion or enemas, use of ligatures, hanging or suspension, or other implements of torture)
- Regular use of degrading or vile words directed at the child victim/witness
- Use of specific behaviors by the defendant (i.e., the victim noting that "he always smoked a cigarette first, and snapped the lighter just before he would come into my room")

Karen, age 8, was molested by her best friend's father, Bob. Bob showed Karen his daughter's pet rabbit one day. Karen was petting the rabbit when Bob took it by the neck, twisted the head, and placed the dead animal carcass in her lap. He proceeded to molest her. Bob told Karen that if she ever told anyone about the abuse, he would break the neck of his daughter, Trisha, and her death would be Karen's fault.

Karen did not reveal the chronic abuse for 7 years because she thought she was saving her best friend's life. Karen was terrified about talking to the police and testifying in court. She needed constant reassurances that Trisha was alive and well throughout the investigative and legal process.

Hostile Courtroom Spectators

Sometimes, there are angry friends or relatives of a defendant who attend court hearings. It is not unusual to find spectators making faces, gestures, or other questionable body movements when witnesses are testifying. Some gestures can be quite subtle and very intimidating to witnesses.

In many courtrooms, attention is focused on the testifying witness only. Observe and pay attention to courtroom spectators when a witness is testifying! A court educator should be looking not only at the child witness but also at the courtroom and spectators. Bailiffs, courtroom clerks, law enforcement personnel, or other professionals should all be trained to observe courtroom spectators and to report any unusual, threatening, or signaling behaviors to the lawyers or judge. The judge can decide on the appropriate course of action.

> Jake was charged with committing several sexual assaults. The child victims said that they were fearful about testifying in court, especially about what Jake's friends might do to them. The children said that they did not know the names of specific people who scared them, but they could point them out if they showed up in court.
>
> On the day of trial, a few child witnesses told the court educator that they saw some of the "scary friends" entering the court building. The court educator asked courtroom authorities to keep careful watch over these people. When the first child was testifying, one of the identified spectators was seen raising his finger to his throat and slowly sliding it from ear to ear. The judge addressed the problem immediately. Had the courtroom personnel not been alert, this serious problem would likely have been completely missed.

Not all hostile courtroom spectators will be from the other side. Supporters for child victims and witnesses sometimes act out in court, too. All people going into a courtroom, no matter their role or relationship with a victim or witness, need to know that they must control their emotions in the courtroom. The father of one child witness was arrested and jailed following this incident:

> The defendant was testifying at his jury trial. The father of a child victim had been seated inside the courtroom throughout the trial. During one

part of the defendant's testimony, the father jumped to his feet, raised his fist, and screamed, "You're lying! He's a fucking liar!"

The case was declared a mistrial, and the father was severely fined and served time in the county jail for this outburst. He was also ordered to pay all the costs for the canceled jury trial, was prohibited from attending the rescheduled trial, and put his child in the position of having to testify again at another trial.

PREPARING A STANDARD SAFETY PLAN

Safety plans should be thought about in advance, before meeting with a child witness and his or her family. Prepare a standard safety plan document to hand out to the parents.

Standard Safety Plan Suggestions

1. Teach young children how to dial 911, and teach them the importance of this number.
2. Tell people whom you trust, such as friends, family, neighbors, and coworkers, what is going on, and talk with them about ways they might be able to help.
3. Memorize the telephone numbers for those whom you may need to reach quickly.
4. Pack a small emergency bag with the following supplies in it:
   - Enough clothing for each member of the family for 3 days
   - Grooming supplies for everyone (toothbrushes, a comb, toothpaste, deodorant, aspirin, antacid, etc.)
   - Enough prescription medicine, in a sealed and labeled container, for 3 days, with the dosage times clearly marked
   - Money (cash), checks, extra house and car keys
   - A duplicate marriage or divorce certificate, custody papers, copy of driver's license, passport, and immunization records for the children
   - A small special toy or stuffed animal for each young child that he or she would find comforting during a crisis

5. Memorize foot and road escape routes from your home and through your neighborhood.

6. Memorize various streets and routes that could get you to a safe location from your home, place of work, children's schools, and your most frequented shopping stores.

OTHER BASIC SAFETY TIPS AND/OR CONSIDERATIONS

Cellular Telephones

Consider temporarily lending cellular telephones to witnesses who have no telephone. Law enforcement agencies, domestic abuse shelters, and victim/witness programs should all have at least one cellular telephone available for emergencies such as this.

Automobile Parking Alternatives

Instruct witnesses to park their automobiles in safe locations. This may mean that they should *not* park in front of their apartment or house or in a residential driveway. Some suggested alternatives could be a neighbor's garage or an obscure parking location within a short (but safe) walking distance from home. Many criminals are lazy. If a vehicle is not readily available for them to tamper with, they usually don't look too far for it.

Dogs

Criminals are frequently deterred by the sound of a large growling dog.[1] Have an adult borrow a friend's large dog for a while, if possible. Dogs with a deep growl that will bark at outdoor sounds are excellent. Use dogs that are unfamiliar with the defendant.

Note

1. Unpublished written communications between the author and several convicted rapists in a maximum security prison (1996).

3

Basic Foundation Information: Communicating With Child Witnesses

Effectively communicating with a child witness will be the most important basic function performed by professionals within the investigative or legal arena. Everything that is done is based upon a clear understanding of each other through communication.

Topics discussed in this chapter are as follows:

> A. Basic information: Facts about children's language skills (by Dr. Anne Graffam Walker)
> B. Potential sources of information about a child witness communication skill or limitation
> C. Communication problems with multiple events or "repeated acts" cases
> D. The need to anchor a witness during a conversation or testimony

Effectively communicating with a child witness is essential. Because of the importance of this issue, included in this segment is some very basic guidance from one of the most respected authorities on forensic linguistics in the field, Dr. Anne Graffam Walker. The following excerpt from Walker (1998) has been reprinted with her permission.

Basic Information: Facts About
Children's Language Skills

In general:

By the age of 3, most children of normal development can string words together in generally correct order, and can use language in a conversationally appropriate way. Their vocabulary can range from about 500 to 3,000 words. They can identify over five parts of their own bodies.

By the age of 5 to 6, the basic language structures of most children are well established, although far from fully mature. They can define SOME simple words. They can accurately name three or four colors. With a receptive vocabulary generally estimated at around 14,000 words, their language sounds on the surface much like an adult's.

This misleading surface similarity of language does not mean, however, that these children have achieved *mastery* of their language. Late acquisitions include (but are not limited to) the ability to handle: (1) complex sentences containing relative (e.g., who, which, that) or adverbial (e.g., when, before, after, while) clauses; (2) some critical verb structures like many passives; (3) complex negation; and (4) structural distinctions such as those between ask and tell, know and think, easy to do (see/ please/ etc.) and hard to do (see, etc.), and some syntactic aspects of the verb "promise"—that is, the way we use the *word* (not the concept of) "promise" in a sentence.

Nor does the apparent similarity mean that children this age have mastered all those concepts *expressed* in language, such as age, time, speed, size, duration and number (How old is she? When did it happen?, How fast was the car going? How big was the knife? How long did it last? How many times did it happen?).

They do not fully understand the family relationships expressed by kinship terms such as parents, aunt, grandfather, cousin.

While recent empirical research with abused children indicates an understanding of the concepts of truth/lie by at least age 5, the ability to *express* or *define* that knowledge (What is truth?) develops much later.

By age 10 to 11, most children have acquired the ability to use most relational words in an adult fashion.

What follows is a list of a few features of language that children acquire from about the age of 2 to 10. Keep in mind that all of these data are for *native speakers of English*. Children (and adults too) who have English as a second language may lag far behind the acquisition ranges given here, so special care must be taken in talking with and listening to them. There is one other caveat to add: Not all studies of children's acquisition are comparable. Some follow only a few children over a long period of time, others observe larger groups of children in shorter bursts of time. The result is that scholars often disagree as to actual acquisition ages. There is, however, a middle ground, and that is what is represented next.

Specific lexical skills:

Feature	Age
Adjectives	
■ Comparatives (e.g., more, bigger, but not deeper, wider, earlier, later)	4-5
■ Superlatives (e.g., most, biggest)	3-6
■ Ability to make complex comparisons in response to questions (e.g., Which box is taller than it is fat?)	6-8
Articles	
■ Full mastery of contrast between "the" and "a"	about 8
Adverbs	
■ Reliable distinction between before/after	7+
■ "Frontwards," "sidewards," "backwards"	about 7
Prepositions	
■ In, on (first two acquired)	1½ to 2½
■ Off, out (of), away (from)	2 to 3
■ Toward, up	3 to 3½
■ In front of, next to, around	3½ to 4
■ Beside	4 to 4½
■ Down	4½ to 5
■ Ahead of, behind	4½ to 5½
Pronouns	
■ Possessives:	
— My, your, mine, his	by age 3½
— Their, her(s), his, its, our(s)	3 to 5
■ Deictic ("pointing") pronouns "this" vs. "That" (when no fixed referent is available)	7+
■ Reliable matching of a pronoun to a following noun (e.g., he . . . John)	about 10
■ Verb contrast between come-go; bring-take	7-8+
■ tell-ask	7-8

WH questions (*WH*at, *WH*ere, *WH*o, *WH*y, How, *WH*en)
- Appear in child's speech (in approximately above order)   from 2½ to 4½
- Appropriate *grammatical* response to WH questions acquired   by age 5½
- Appropriate *cognitive* response to *WH*y, How, *WH*en   by about age 10

Syntactic Skills
- Passives: with action verbs (e.g., hit, push: Were you hit?)   age 5+
- With all verbs, including non-action (e.g., Were you liked by)   7-13+
- "Tag" questions (e.g., Xxx, *isn't it*(tag underlined), produced at about age 4+
- Combined with negatives in the assertion, (e.g., That's*not* what she
  said; isn't that so?/is that not so?) is confusing on into adulthood.

Conversational Skills
- Turn Taking: from first use to mastery   before age 2 to 6+
- Asking contingent questions   by age 3
  (Contingent questions relate to the immediately prior utterance;
  e.g., questions which indicate that something just said is not fully
  understood, such as "What did you say?")
- Ability to report the basic elements of typical events (such as what
  happens at a birthday party)   age 3
- Ability to describe, narrate, and inform in adult-satisfactory way   May be still
                                                                        developing in
                                                                        jr. and sr. high
                                                                        school years.[1]

The ages given above represent approximations only of the time when each feature is fully and reliably acquired, meaning that the child can both comprehend and produce the feature. Of course, children reach different stages at individual times that can vary widely. Acquisition of these features is also apparently retarded by as much as 12 to 18 months if the child has been abused.

Court educators will find out that lawyers and judges will be interested in learning about the abilities, limitations, or special difficulties any witness may have because they need to solicit accurate and complete information (testimony) from them.

Although law offices or courts may refer children to child assessment specialists or child psychologists (who have trained in forensics) to perform the task of assessing a child's capabilities to meet the expectations of the criminal justice system, and cope with doing so, most jurisdictions do not have the resources or money to do so.

If, at any time, a child appears to be having emotional, developmental, or psychological difficulty during the meetings with a court educator or lawyer, it is strongly encouraged that a skilled psychology professional be consulted immediately. (See mental health discussion in Chapter 5.)

Most child witnesses will be fine. But all child witnesses will require an investment of time. Very young children, cognitively or developmentally impaired children, or severely traumatized children will require an even greater investment of time for adequate court education and preparation.

Potential Sources of Information About a Child Witness Communication Skill or Limitation

Excellent sources of information about a child's communication abilities are the forensic interviewer, detective, or the child's social workers. In addition, court educators may consider, when appropriate and necessary, approaching a (frequently overlooked) professional for specific and direct information about a child's cognitive or linguistic abilities and/or limitations—the child's schoolteacher. If approved, the case lawyer could prepare a release so that the teacher could release certain information about the child.

Use caution. Be clear that you are seeking only specific information about a particular child's developmental and cognitive abilities or limitations in order to communicate effectively with the court educator, lawyers, or judge. *No additional information should be sought about any child witness.* The purpose for the release of this information is only to assist with communicating appropriately with the child. Discuss this issue with the case lawyer before tendering such a release to a parent for his or her signature.

Communication Problems With Multiple Events or "Repeated Acts" Cases

Multiple and repeated criminal acts that occur over an extended period of time can be problematic for many victims. Communicating about multiple events with a child witness should be done carefully. Times, dates, and duration of specific acts can be difficult to separate and recall with exact specificity. An example of an opening statement to a jury amplifies the difficulty a child may have when multiple criminal acts are being charged:

> "Ladies and gentlemen, the case you are going to hear involves the sexual assault of 9-year-old Traci, from the time she turned 6 until last Christmas. Although there were dozens of incidents over the years, the defendant is specifically charged with only four of them. The reason for this is because of the confusion and lack of recalled details for many of the assaults, for this defendant had a sexual routine, and it is very hard for Traci to tell us about each and every time she was abused.
>
> Traci remembers many details about the first and last incidents—and two others—because of events that occurred on those dates. I am going to ask you to use your common sense when listening to this case. Try to understand how difficult recalling the dates and details has been for Traci and why she recalls details about some incidents and not others, yet they did happen. I ask you to think to yourselves about your own sexual experiences during the past year. Can you recall all of the details of your last six sexual encounters? Where you were when you had sex the fourth to the last time? What time of day it was? What you were wearing? What you had for dinner? What exact words were said?"

The Need to Anchor a Witness During a Conversation or Testimony

Children may need assistance with focusing on one event at a time. It can be very difficult and frustrating for children to separate, or narrate in sequence, multiple events or topics. Children may appear inconsistent or confused when talking about, and later being cross-examined about, multiple events. One method of helping a child witness to stay focused on which event is being discussed is to anchor the witness by helping him or her to visually separate the events.

Anchors can be anything visual, such as a photograph, drawing, toy, or object. An anchor is whatever will focus a child's attention on a specific incident, event, or topic being discussed. The following is an example of how anchoring took place during a child's testimony:

> Jordan, age 5, was the victim of multiple abusive activities in several locations. One incident involved Jordan having a green pickle inserted into his anus. Another incident involved a rag, soaked with some odorous substance, being placed in his mouth while he was beaten.

During court preparation with the lawyer, Jordan and the court educator drew pictures of a pickle, rag, carpet, bed, and mattress, as well as the
houses in which the crimes occurred. Jordan drew the pictures just like he
wanted them. The case detective took Polaroid photographs of the actual
houses involved and had them enlarged. One house was blue, and another
house was red.

During his testimony, Jordan identified what the pictures depicted and
identified the photographs of the houses. The items were marked as exhibits. When the lawyer asked Jordan questions about a specific event, the
picture was exhibited before Jordan that had previously been matched
with the event (by the child witness).

When the lawyer changed the topic or event to be discussed, he also
changed the picture at which Jordan was looking. This clear visual signal
helped Jordan to focus on what topic was being discussed and greatly re-
duced his confusion (and likely the confusion of the jurors as well).

The following conversation is an example of the above anchoring:

Q: Jordan, we are going to talk about the time something happened
with a pickle. (Jordan's drawing of the pickle was shown to him.)

A: Okay.

Q: Jordan, I'm sorry. I need to ask you something else before we talk
about the pickle. (The lawyer removes the picture of the pickle and
replaces it with a photograph of the red house.) I want to ask you
something else about what happened at the red house.

A: Okay.

This visual change and verbal topic change by the lawyer helped this
child to understand which events(s) were being discussed. The child
was able to easily discuss numerous events in this manner without becoming confused.

Note

1. References upon which the above information is based are as follows:

Bloom, L. 1991. *Language development from two to three.* NY: Cambridge University
Press.

Brown, R. 1973. *A first language: The early stages* Cambridge, MA: Harvard University Press.

Clark, E.V. 1998. Personal communication.

Clark, E.V. & O.K. Garnica. 1974. Is he coming or going? On the acquisition of deictic verbs. *Journal of Verbal Learning & Verbal Behavior,* 13:559-572.

Clark, H.H. & E.V. Clark. 1977. *Psychology and language.* NY: Harcourt Brace Jovanovich.

Garvey, C. 1975. Requests and responses in children's speech. *Journal of Child Language,* 2:41-63.

Horgan, D. 1978. The development of the full passive. *Journal of Child Language,* 5:65-80.

Leonard, L.B. (1984). Normal language acquisition: Some recent findings and clinical implications. In Holland, A. (Ed.), *Language disorders in children: Recent advances,* pp. 1-36. San Diego: College-Hill Press.

Lennenberg, E.H. 1967. *Biological foundations of language.* NY: Wiley.

Lyon, T.D. & K.J. Saywitz. (Forthcoming). Young maltreated children's competence to take the oath. *Applied Developmental Science.*

Mordecai, Palin, Palmer. 1982. LINQUEST Language Sample Analysis, Linquest Software Inc.

Reich, P.A. 1986. *Language development.* Englewood Cliffs, NJ: Prentice-Hall.

Romaine, S. 1984. *The language of children and adolescents.* NY: Basil Blackwell.

Taylor, M.G. & P.B. Purfall. 1987. A developmental analysis of directional terms frontwards, backwards, and sidewards. Paper presented at the meeting of the Society for Research in Child Development, Baltimore, MD.

Warren, A.R. & L.A. McCloskey. 1993. Pragmatics: Language in social contexts. In Berko Gleason, J. (Ed.), *The development of language* 3d Ed. NY: Macmillan.

Wood, B.S. 1981. *Children and communication: verbal and nonverbal language development.* Englewood Cliffs, NJ: Prentice-Hall, Inc.

4

Meeting the Parent and Child

After foundation preparation has been completed by the court educator, he or she is ready to make the first contact with the parents or caregiver and the child victim or witness.

Topics discussed in this chapter are as follows:

A. Meeting the parent
1. First contact—introductions
2. Scheduling appointments
3. Meeting the parent
4. Meeting the child
5. Moving from the waiting area to the work location
B. Working with the child
1. Hands off!
2. Separating the parent and child
3. Education and assessment
   a. Building rapport—a few tips about talking with children
   b. Work and no-work time rules
   c. Telling the truth—will the child be able to take an oath?
   d. Making mistakes
   e. Correcting mistakes
   f. Guessing at answers
   g. Permission to repeat certain words
   h. Answering out loud, saying "yes and no," and the use of a microphone
   i. Repeated questions
   j. Hard questions—time/numbers/distance/measurements
   k. Kinship relationships
   l. Common words used in court
   m. Asking for a break
   n. Reducing anxiousness—use of rocks, coins, representational dolls, breathing exercises

o. Courtroom layout—drawing model miniature courtroom
p. Tour of an actual courtroom (and exits)
q. Closing the appointment
r. Other common questions
s. A subpoena from the other lawyer
t. What to wear to court
u. Sequestration rules
C. Debriefing, celebrating efforts, the verdict, and sentencing
   1. Debriefing after testimony is completed
   2. Celebrating the child's efforts
   3. The verdict
   4. Sentencing
      a. Presentence investigative reports
      b. Victim impact statements
   5. Thank you letters

Meeting the Parent

FIRST CONTACT—INTRODUCTIONS

The first contact with a parent is very important and will likely be done by telephone. It is difficult to know how much time a parent will need during this initial contact. Some parents will have many questions for you, whereas other parents will ask little of you. Try to avoid being interrupted during this first contact with a parent. First impressions are very important, and interruptions to your conversation could make the parent/listener feel unimportant.

Introduce yourself to the parent. Explain who you are, what your job is, and how you will be helpful to him or her and the child. Ask the parent what he or she would like to know. Do your best to let the parent know the status of their particular case, and discuss issues of concern (e.g., safety, worries, or fear, as identified in Part 2). Let the parent know that you have some literature available that may be helpful for him or her and the child. Ask if he or she would like the information sent to him or her.

Printed material for witnesses and parents should be age-appropriate and written in a manner that will be easily understood by the intended recipient. (Jurisdictions with populations who have English as a second language should attempt to have literature prepared in that person's primary language.) Suggested materials for mailing could include the following:

- A child's workbook, court-related coloring book, or other documents that explain, in general terms, something about the court process
- Adult document providing basic court-related information and definitions
- General information for parents (see Appendix B for a sample informational document titled "When Your Child Goes to Court: How Parents Can Help")
- Case identification information (file number, lawyer names, judge name)
- Safety tip information, if appropriate
- Information brochures, crime victim compensation benefit forms, and any other appropriate community or mental health information that could be of benefit to the parents

Leaving Messages

Leave a brief identifying message for parents who are not home, but have an answering machine. Leave your name, who you are, a telephone number, and a selection of times for them to call you back. Let the parents know that you are sending some general information to them in the mail, but wish to talk with them in person as soon as it is convenient.

Parents with no telephone should receive a short letter of introduction stating the above information. Let parents know that it is important to talk with them and to please try to connect with you by telephone, by letter, or in person. List a variety of dates, times, and ways for them to reach you.

Most parents will be quite pleased to hear from you and will reach you within a day or two after receiving their information. Many parents will be very protective of their child and may initially appear anxious and cautious. This reaction is normal and should be expected. Parents need to know that their child is going to be in very capable and competent hands during the pendency of any court action, so it is important to develop a bond of mutual trust and open communication with them.

Remember, during this first contact, the parents are "checking you out," and you want their first impression to be as positive as possible.

Once the parents know who you are and how you are going to be of assistance to them and their child, make sure they understand how you can be reached with any future questions or concerns. Consider providing the parents with a listing of your regular work hours, as well as the names and telephone numbers for alternate people whom they could contact in case of a crisis or emergency.

Some children require a small amount of time for court education and preparation before testifying at a court hearing. Other children may need significantly more time before they are ready and able to go to court. In some cases, this amount of time could be several weeks or months. It is suggested that a court educator meet with a child witness and his or her parents well in advance of a hearing date to assess the needs of a child witness and to gauge the amount of time that will be required to adequately prepare the child to testify.

Court educators should try to have some contact with a child witness and a parent before a charge is issued (by a prosecutor). This is especially important if the witness is very young or traumatized, or if there are identifiable special needs that must be addressed.

Forensic interviewers, law enforcement investigators, case social workers, or therapists are excellent information sources who could immediately alert a lawyer or court educator to special, unique, or problematic circumstances that should prompt a meeting with the court educator, lawyer, and child to assess his or her needs before a charging decision is made.

SCHEDULING APPOINTMENTS

Try to accomplish as much as possible during the initial conversation with the parents as well as during the first visit with the parents and child. This may include incorporating a first meeting with the case lawyer during or following the educational session with the child. To accomplish this, consider the following:

1. Secure a variety of dates and times that allow both the educator and case lawyer to meet with a child witness.

- ◆ Schedule a meeting session with the parents and child.
- ◆ Let the parents select the date(s) and time(s) that work out best for them.
- ◆ During the first telephone contact, let the parents know what will be taking place during the educational meeting with the child, and enlist their assistance with first introductions.
- ◆ Talk with the parents about the need for them to gently separate during the educational process, if possible. Explain how to best accomplish exiting the area, or what to do if the child appears uncomfortable during this process.

2. Prearrange a meeting between the parents and the case lawyer. If the parents are able to separate from their child, they can then meet with the lawyer. This private meeting will give the parents and the lawyer some time to get to know each other without the child being present. Be patient and flexible with this step, for it is important to not separate the child and parent too soon.

3. Provide the parents with directions to the meeting location, and include parking information.

4. Inform the parents that you expect them to have a number of important questions, but that they may not want to call each time a question arises. Instruct them to write down nonurgent questions and to bring the list with them to the initial meeting. Remind the parents that it is perfectly okay to call with urgent or troubling questions, rather than waiting for the appointment date.

The court educator and lawyer will need to divide the allotment of time with the child and parents as deemed appropriate and necessary. If the court educator meets the child first, he or she could introduce the child and parents to the lawyer. The court educator may remain with the child during this meeting to continue building an emotional and educational bond with the child.

Some children comfortably handle meeting and working with two separate professionals during their first session. Other children become too tired. Most children will easily tolerate these work sessions, especially when regular 5- to 10-minute play and work breaks are taken. Children as young as age 3 have tolerated up to 1-hour educational sessions comfortably. Carefully observe and listen to the child. Look for signs of fatigue. If a child is becoming restless, fussy, or tired, end the session and reschedule for another day.

MEETING THE PARENT

The first time you meet with a parent and child, be positive and be on time. Don't keep parents or child witnesses waiting longer than 5 minutes. Be positive with your approach, and shake the hands of the parents as you introduce yourself as "their court friend and court teacher." (The child will be listening and paying attention, even if he or she appears distracted.) The use of the word "friend" is gentle and kind, and almost all children have fond thoughts about teachers. Even very young children have likely learned that the word "friend" is something okay and nice, and that teachers help people to learn about things.

MEETING THE CHILD

Out of courtesy and respect, you approach the parent first, but have a puppet on one hand. Be prepared to use the puppet to greet the child. Gauge your approach to a child by observing the response and demeanor of the child when you are greeting and talking with the parents.

Greet the child by going down to his or her eye level. Show the puppet during the greeting, but maintain a physical distance from the child. Introduce the child to the puppet, and then let the child know your first name. Inform the child that you are going to be his or her court friend and teacher, too.

MOVING FROM THE WAITING
AREA TO THE WORK LOCATION

Do not ask a child if he or she wants to go with you to "the child room." Some children will say no to this question. A negative response will immediately frustrate efforts to begin working with the child. It is recommended that the court educator invite the parents and child to the work area by saying: "Follow me, please. We're going to go to our children's room to talk." Open the door or gesture the direction for everyone. Children rarely refuse to go to a location referred to as "the kids' room" or "the children's area" when invited to do so.

If a child resists leaving, don't force him or her to move or relocate to another area. If the parents cannot politely get the child to move to the work area, reschedule the appointment for another time and try again. Children should not be forced or made to cooperate. Work with the parents to try to discover what was bothering the child, and attempt to remedy the situation if at all possible. Sometimes, a brief first visit, followed by a second visit, is all that is needed to make a child more comfortable and cooperative.

With cooperative children, proceed with moving the child and parents to a quiet or private work area. With shy or hesitant children, engage in more friendly conversation with the parents first, and enlist their cooperation with relocating from a waiting room to the work area:

> "Mrs. Jones, I just happen to have some boxes of new crayons and paper in our children's room. We also have some wonderful new books. Come over and see them!" As you direct them by walking slowly to the location, continue speaking with the parents by saying something like, "Does Amy like to color?" Usually, the parent will ask the child if he or she likes to color. Sometimes, this question prompts the child to answer by him- or herself.

Another icebreaker has been the use of books with audio sound buttons that are pressed during the reading of the story. Most children easily accept playing with these books.

Working With the Child

HANDS OFF!

Child witnesses should be approached with respect and should not be physically touched. Invading a child's personal space happens far too often by well-intentioned people. Many people forget to view this meeting through the eyes of a child. The following two examples serve to remind us about physical approaches to children:

> A 6-foot tall, 180-pound lawyer approached a 4-year-old child. The lawyer rushed to the child in his usual friendly manner, causing the child to with-

draw and hide. The lawyer did not consider that he appeared as a fast-moving giant to this child. What would you do if a stranger who was three times your height and weight came rushing directly at you?

A lawyer named Quinlan was preparing to meet a 9-year-old boy for the first time. The child, Jason, was the victim of a grooming child molester named Erik. Erik began grooming Jason for sex over a long period of time. The touches started with simple back and shoulder rubs, progressed to thigh massages, and then went on to fellatio.

When Jason arrived at the courthouse to meet Quinlan for the first time, Quinlan shook hands with Jason's father, and then told the father to wait while he took Jason to his office to talk. As Jason walked toward the lawyer's office, Quinlan began, in a friendly manner, rubbing Jason's shoulder and back. Jason appeared pale and stiff as he entered Quinlan's office. Jason sat in a chair with his feet curled around the legs of the chair and his hands tightly gripping the arm rests. Jason was silent and unresponsive with Quinlan.

Quinlan ultimately asked for assistance from another staff member (who maintained a respectful physical distance from Jason, gained his trust, and gradually developed a rapport with him). Quinlan learned a valuable lesson about placing his hands on a child's body, no matter how innocent and well-intentioned the touch was.

SEPARATING THE PARENT AND CHILD

Most children will not immediately separate from their parents when meeting a new person for the first time. This is especially true if the child is also meeting this new person for the first time in a foreign environment.

Young children, usually under the age of 8, require more time and possibly extra visits before they are ready to separate from the parents to work with the court educator or lawyer alone. The need for multiple meetings is why it is important for court educators and lawyers to make contact with children and parents well in advance of any anticipated court hearing.

Make arrangements with the parents (discussed with them during earlier contacts) to *slowly* withdraw from the work area when the child appears to be ready for this step. It may be necessary for the parents to step out of the room but stay in viewing distance. The parents gradually withdraw from the area only if the child does not object.

Never force a child to separate from the parents, and never have parents just disappear, for this causes great anxiety, panic, and mistrust. If this process is done gently and respectfully, most children will eventually separate.

For children who cannot or will not separate from the parents, it will be necessary to conduct all of the educational and preparation work with the parents present. Situations like this prompt special pretrial motion considerations, such as the need to have the parents testify before the child so that they can be present with their child when he or she testifies.

EDUCATION AND ASSESSMENT

Building Rapport

When meeting a child, it is important to try to develop some rapport and to begin building a trusting relationship. Frame this experience for the child. In other words, let the child know why he or she is with you now. One method might be to ask the child a question, such as, "Do you know why you are here with me?" Some children may know and will say yes. If they say yes, ask them why they think they are with you. Other children will have no idea why they are with you, and you need to try to explain this to them in a way they can understand:

> "Cindy, people go to court for lots of reasons. They go to a special room called a courtroom. In the courtroom, people talk to special people. Some of the special people in court will be a judge, some lawyers, and some other people. The lawyers ask lots of questions. My job is to tell you all about court. I am also going to tell you about all the special people who may be in court with you. I know you talked to (police, a social worker, etc.) about something you saw or heard, or that happened to you. I am not going to ask you about that. The lawyer(s) will ask you about that. I'm going to tell you about going to court. You can ask me questions, too, okay?"

Show the child the immediate surroundings, and let the child look around. One way to begin communicating with a child is to use an easel with paper and crayons. Write your name on the paper. Invite the child to write his or her name on the paper. Many children will immediately start drawing or writing.

Other children may need to have a short story read to them, or to work with you on putting a simple puzzle together in order to start a dialogue. What is important is to get the child to talk with you.

Here are some reminders and other tips about talking with children:

- Use simple words, such as "talk" instead of "testify" or "tell" instead of "describe."
- Try to use as few words as possible in any sentence or question.
- Refrain from asking "do you remember" questions. (To remember something is a task one needs to learn, and even older school-age children have difficulty with this task.)
- Avoid asking questions that require a yes or no answer. Ask questions that require a narrative response so that you can be more assured that the child understands what was asked of him or her.
- Use the proper names of people when talking with witnesses, rather than using pronouns like "he," "she," "them," or "they." For example, ask "What did *Karen* say?" rather than "What did *she* say?"
- Have one thought in each question.

Work Time and No-Work Time Rules

Most children have heard the word "rules." Games that children play usually have rules. Let the child know that there are some rules about your work, and there are rules about court, too. "My job is to teach you the court rules."

Children have limited attention spans and need frequent breaks. Explain to the child that you will be able to do some fun things during the no-work period, and that you will be working to learn different things about court during the work time. Divide the education room or area into no-work and work zones. The reason for this space division is to help the child see that there is a difference between work and no-work activities.

Show the child a timer with a bell. Set the timer for 5 minutes. Let the child know that you will both do something that is fun and no work for 5 minutes. When the bell goes off, tell the child that it is now work time, reset the timer, and move to the work area. The space between the work and no-work area does not have to be large, but it should be distinct.

The timing of the bell may be increased or decreased for work or no-work time, as deemed necessary. Children quickly learn what the bell means and will switch tasks easily.

During the educational process, it will be important for the child to learn that there is only work time when in court, but that there will be no-work time when court is done.

Telling the Truth—Will the Child Witness Be Able to Take an Oath?

Taking an oath presupposes that one understands what it means to tell the truth, and that one appreciates one's obligations to tell the truth when promising to do so. If a young child does not understand the difference between the truth and lies or fails to appreciate the obligation to tell the truth, he or she may be found incompetent. The competence questions are not designed to assess the likelihood that a child is suggestible or prone to lie. Rather, they determine whether the child is qualified to promise to tell the truth; that is, that he or she knows the difference between truth and lies and appreciates his or her obligation to tell the truth (Lyon, 1996).

The great majority of children, even as young as age 3, understand the difference between truth and falsehood and appreciate their duty to tell the truth in court. Still, moral behavior does not always follow directly from moral reasoning, so judges must take care to explain to children the importance of relating the facts as they actually happened (Perry & Wrightsman, 1991):

Judge: Okay. I am going to ask you some questions, okay?
Child: Okay.
Judge: Do you get in trouble for not telling the truth at home?
Child: Yea.
Judge: What happens if you don't tell the truth at home?
Child: I get time-out.
Judge: What is time-out?

Child: Sit in the corner for a long time and I don't get to do nothin'.

Judge: Would you get in trouble if you don't tell me the truth?

Child: Yea.

(The court bailiff gave the witness a cup of water. The judge asked the child the following):

Judge: If I told you that this man (pointing and smiling at the bailiff) just gave you some M&Ms, would that be the truth or a lie?

Child: A lie.

Judge: What would be the truth?

Child: He didn't give me M&Ms. He gave me water (taking a sip).

Judge: What happens when people don't tell me the truth?

Child: Oh, they get in big trouble. They can't watch Power Rangers anymore! That's a really good show.

(Laughter.)

Judge: I need to make sure that people only tell me the truth. What really happened. Will you promise to tell me the truth today?

Child: Yes.

Although this was a humorous exchange from an adult standpoint, the child was serious. The court found that the child in this case understood the difference between the truth and a lie. The child was also able to articulate that there would be some likely punishment for telling a lie, and affirmatively agreed to tell the truth.

Making Mistakes

Children need to know that they can correct any mistake they have made in court by saying so, and saying so right away. Children should understand that they can make corrections about what they have said and not get into trouble for doing so. Children need to know that adults may make mistakes in court, and that he or she has permission to correct any mistake he or she hears.

Correcting Mistakes

Children should know that they need to be completely truthful, and that it is okay, and right, to correct any mistakes made by anyone in the courtroom, even adults.

The dialogue above demonstrated that the child witness was able to tell the judge that he was not given M&Ms, because that was a lie. The child stated that he had water. This child corrected the judge, a very powerful person. The fact that the child witness was able to correct a judge about a mistake could indicate that the child is not intimidated by the adults in the courtroom, is more likely to correct any misinformation, and is likely to be careful when responding to a question. That child also attained a certain level of credibility because of his precise and articulate responses.

Guessing at Answers

Some children worry about not knowing an answer to a question. Some children think that they are supposed to have an answer to every question an adult asks (believing that an adult would not ask a question if he or she didn't think the child knew the answer). Unfortunately, this confusion may cause a child to guess at an answer.

Children need to learn that they may not know the answers to all of the questions asked, and that it is okay to not know all the answers. Tell children that they should not guess at an answer. Rather, they should say they don't know, if they really do not know an answer. For example,

Q: How many stars are in the sky?
A: I don't know!

When the child said, "I don't know," he or she should be told that he or she did the right thing by saying he or she did not know the answer. Inform children that it is all right to not know answers to some questions.

Let the child know that he or she will be asked a lot of questions. Children need to be taught that if a question is asked, and they do not understand the question, they need to say so to the person who asked the question. To demonstrate this to the child, the court educator could ask obvious questions that the child will not understand:

Q: Wendy, do you have a *ra-zen-fra-zen*?
A: What's that?
Q: Don't you know what that is?

A: No, I don't know.

Q: Those are good answers! I don't know what a *ra-zen-frat-zen* is either. I just wanted you to know that it is okay to say you don't know or understand something.

The more fun your questions are, the more likely the child is going to get the message, and he or she will also have an enjoyable time learning the rules.

Some children may know an answer to a question but are hesitant or won't want to talk about it. Let children know that they should

- Say they know an answer when they truthfully do know the answer.
- Say they *do not* know an answer when they really do not know the answer.

Tell children that there is a difference between not knowing an answer and really knowing the answer, but just not being ready or willing to talk about it. If this situation is not clarified for children, some of them may say they do not know something when they do know, but they don't want to talk about it and are unable to find a way to express their dilemma.

Try to determine why a child may not want to answer a particular question, and what could help make him or her more comfortable and willing to answer. Some children will indicate that they would feel more comfortable whispering an answer to the lawyer, and the lawyer could say the word out loud. Other children may be willing to write down an answer instead. (When this has been done, the lawyer repeats the word and verifies the accuracy of it with the child. The court record reflects this exchange and what takes place.)

Permission to Repeat Certain Words

As stated above, some children won't answer a question asked of them because they worry about repeating certain words. This is especially true if the words used by someone and heard by the child are words that are unacceptable in their home environment. When reviewing reports or talking with a witness, be sure to give him or her permission to use the *exact* words used by anyone:

> Juliana whispered to the detective, "Oliver said, 'Fuck me!' " Juliana then asked the detective if her mother would hear what she just said. When the detective told Juliana that her mother would hear those words at some point in time, she started to cry. Juliana was worried that her mother would be mad at her for saying bad words, but exclaimed, "I didn't say them, *he* did!"

The court educator needs to inform parents about the anxiety some children experience over this issue, and how important it is, legally, to have an accurate report of events and statements.

Answering out Loud, Saying "Yes / No," and the Use of a Microphone

Children need to understand that they must answer questions out loud. Explain the function of a court reporter, who needs to hear what is recorded. Demonstrate how a court reporter cannot hear someone nodding or shaking his or her head.

Children should learn to use the proper words of "yes" and "no," instead of slang responses such as "yea," "uh-huh," "nah," "uh-uh," or "um-hum."

Many courtrooms are small enough to easily hear a child witness talk in a normal tone of voice; however, other rooms are too large, and a child's timid voice may not be heard. Instruct witnesses to speak in a normal tone of voice. If a room is going to have a microphone in it, allow the witness to try this device beforehand so that the novelty has worn off.

Repeated Questions

Children need to know that lawyers may ask a lot of questions. Sometimes, the lawyers will ask the same question over and over. Explain to witnesses that they may sometimes need to be very patient with lawyers because they may forget that they already asked a question. Just answer the question as many times as it is asked.

Children need to know that just because a question is asked over and over again does not mean that any earlier answer was wrong. Tell children that some lawyers just want to ask the same questions over and over, and that it is okay for them to do that.

Hard Questions: Time/Numbers/Distance/Measurements

Lawyers frequently ask questions that involve the difficult concepts of time, numbers, or distances.

It is quite common for lawyers to ask witnesses to describe some distance (or near/far) or time-related questions, such as, How far away was he? How long did that last? How many times did that happen?

To answer these questions, a witness will need to have the developmental skills to understand, process, calculate, and respond appropriately. Many of these skills are not fully mastered until preadolescence or adolescence, and even some adults cannot answer them properly.

Time. Find out whether a child witness is able to tell time by the clock:

Lawyer: What time did he come to your house?
Child: I don't know.
Lawyer: Was it morning, afternoon, or night?
Child: Just before I went to bed. It was dark.

Will the child be able to differentiate seconds from minutes, hours, days, weeks, or months? A common response to questions is to say something lasted "a few minutes." It is important to ascertain whether or not this witness understands how long a minute actually lasts, as opposed to several seconds.

Numbers. Can this child count? How high can he or she count? Is the child reciting numbers by rote (script memory)? Does the child understand what a number actually represents?

In court, a child responded to a number question as follows:

Q: How old are you?
A: Four (holds up four fingers).

Q: Can you count to 10?

A: Un huh. 1-2-3-4-5-6-7-8-9-10!

Q: That's good. Now, how many times did daddy hit mommy?

A: Five. (Holding up two fingers). She cried and bleeded.

Q: Two times or five times?

A: Four. I'm going to be five.

This child was able to count to 10 by rote (memory). Reciting the words to a song is also something she is likely to be able to do, too. Being able to recite words or numbers does not mean she understands what the song is about or what the number represents. This child did not know how many times the father struck the mother and should not have been asked the question "how many times." This child did, however, appear to have information to share about what she saw of the event.

Consider playing the common, nonthreatening game of "Simon Says" with a child as a way to assess his or her ability to understand and comprehend questions. This game is one in which the caregiver or other people in a room can also participate. Take turns with the child at being the person directing the tasks. Many children will enjoy engaging in the following tasks when done in a friendly and enjoyable manner:

Simon Says: "Pick up *three* pencils."

Simon Says: "Stand on *one* foot."

Simon Says: "Hop for *10 seconds*."

Distance/Height/Measurements. Does this child understand space/distance questions? Can this child demonstrate what an inch, foot, or yard looks like? Does the child have the ability to estimate height or size?

Children are likely to be asked questions about distances both near and far. Distance questions can be very difficult for adults to answer, and they are especially problematic for most children. Determine whether or not a particular child witness can comprehend distance questions.

The following are examples of common, difficult, and poorly asked questions (including examples of multiple questions contained in what is meant to be a single question):

- "How *far away* were you from the car when you first saw it?" (Confusing question—what part of the question is the child to answer?)
- "Was she as *close* to you as I am standing here, or *farther* away?" (How is a child to answer this question?)
- "Can you tell me *how tall* the person was? Was he taller than me, shorter than me, or about the same size?" (Is this a multiple choice question or four questions in one?)
- "Was there any *space* between you and the wall, like a few *inches* or about a *foot?*" (The child witness sat mute. He later said he thought he was being asked something about someone's foot.)

Kinship Questions

Until approximately age 10, children may have difficulty identifying relationships. It is quite common for children to refer to a close friend of the family as "Aunt Rhonda" or "Uncle Pete," yet there may not be any blood relationship between them. It is common for children to be asked in court something like, "How do you know Rhonda is your aunt?"

Some children think the word "aunt" is part of a person's name—the first name is Aunt and the last name is Rhonda. Aunt Rhonda. Many school-aged children have no idea what a cousin is, or how to determine that relationship.

Common Words and People
a Child Is Likely to Meet

Listed below are some words that are commonly used in court. It is important for the lawyers to know whether or not the witness understands what the words mean. Discuss these words with child witnesses. Document what a child says or how a child responds to the following terms, and share this information with the lawyer or judge, whichever is appropriate in your jurisdiction. The lawyer will determine how to best handle communication deficiencies or limitations of a particular witness. This information could be very helpful for the filing of specific motions to limit—or use—certain words in court:

- Over
- Under

- Beside
- Next to
- On top of
- Right or wrong
- Far and near

Have the child do the following exercises (with some tools or props):

1. Step *over* the ball.
2. Put the toy telephone *under* the chair.
3. Come sit *beside* me.
4. Place the book *next to* the white cup.
5. Place the yellow block *on top of* the blue book.
6. If I said you were 14 years old (the child is 7), would I be *right* or *wrong?*
7. What would be the *right* answer to that question?
8. Point to an object some distance away. Ask the child if it is *far away* or *near*. Next, point to something close and ask the question again.

Before and *after* are also common words used in court. Frequently, lawyers ask *before* and *after* questions about a witnessed event. Some children may be able to use the words correctly, and in the proper context, but will not comprehend what is really being asked.

The following exchange is an example of how *before* and *after* was used in court:

A child saw someone get hit by a car on July 10. The child's birthday is July 15. This court hearing was held in October.

Q: Do you know the date that this happened?
A: Ahhh, nope.
Q: When is your birthday?
A: July 15.
Q: Did this thing happen *before* or *after* your birthday?
A: Before.
Q: Are you sure it was *before* your birthday?
A: Yes. I got a bike for my birthday. This happened when I didn't have my bike.

During the educational process, it is important to ensure that the child
has an understanding about whom all the people are that he or she will
encounter, as well as some of the court-related words he or she will
hear.

A researcher named Karen Saywitz (1989) asked some young children to define legal terms such as *court, jury, charges,* and so on. She discovered that many children demonstrated a significant lack of understanding about those words in a legal sense. Some children thought that
"court was a place to play basketball," a jury is "the stuff you wear on
your neck and finger, like a ring," and that "charges are what you do
with your credit card."

Be prepared to list common job positions as well as common court
words that a child witness will likely hear, and talk about them. Some of
these words are unique to the criminal justice system, whereas other
words are heard but have a very different meaning from what they could
mean inside a courtroom. If you are unsure what the above common
court words mean, talk with your local prosecutor, judge, or other legal
resources to clarify proper definitions or explanations to be given child
witnesses in your community. Some typical court people, court jobs, or
court-related words that a child witness should learn are the following:

- Judge
- Jury
- Lawyer, defense attorney, prosecutor, guardian ad litem, county
  attorney, state's attorney
- Court reporter
- Court clerk
- Bailiff
- Witness
- Minor
- Objection, overruled, sustained
- Testify, testimony
- Evidence
- Defendant, respondent, petition, petitioner, parties

- Criminal complaint
- Hearsay
- Sequestration

Explain how the listed words may be used in a courtroom. Tell children how some words could have different meanings, yet sound alike or similar (e.g., minor and miner). Let the child know that he or she can ask you about *any* word that is heard and not understood.

Asking for a Break

Children should receive regular short breaks when testifying, but this is frequently forgotten. Children need to be taught about how to tell the lawyers or judge when he or she needs a break. Some children will readily indicate, "I need to go to the bathroom," or ask, "May I get a drink of water?" Other children may be more comfortable raising a hand to ask permission to have a stretch break. Let the child know about all the various ways in which he or she can indicate needing something.

A child should be permitted to exercise some small amount of control over the environment and not be made to feel as though he or she is a hostage in the courtroom. Break requests should be granted immediately by judges, or at least very quickly after being made.

The court educator should be with the child during breaks to provide support to the child, tend to his or her needs, ensure his or her physical safety, and make sure that no discussion takes place between the child and any unauthorized person if sequestration has been ordered.

Reducing Anxiousness: Use of Rocks, Coins, Representational Dolls, and Breathing Exercises

Witnesses are likely to be nervous when they go to court and may fidget or have difficulty concentrating. People frequently complain that they don't know what to do with their hands when testifying. Give children something small that they can hold in their hands or have in a pocket while testifying, such as a coin, rock, or their special representational doll that they made. Some courts permit children to carry a favorite stuffed animal or even wear a baseball mitt when testifying.

When people are anxious, they tend to start breathing shallowly, using only the upper part of their lungs. Show people how to calm themselves by taking in slow, deep breaths of air.

Courtroom Layout: Drawings, Cardboard or Model
Miniature Courtroom, and a Replica of a Judge's Robe

Show a child witness a model miniature courtroom, drawing of a courtroom, or a cardboard box that is set up to depict a courtroom. It is not necessary to be an artist. Children appreciate attempts to show what a courtroom may look like. A depiction of a courtroom, whether a model or a drawing, is a nonthreatening way to ease a child into an actual tour of a real courtroom.

In addition to using a model or sketched courtroom, a child-size replica judge robe is also a suggested tool to use. The wearing of a replica judge robe goes a long way toward demystifying the judge. Children should be permitted to wear the replica robe during work time as well as on their tour of the real courtroom.

One child, who was very apprehensive during the initial educational process, revealed a stunning fear about court and the judge. While examining the model miniature courtroom, she was looking around the pieces for "the bad room."

When the court educator asked the child what she was talking about, she whispered:

> Robert told me that if I told, the police was gonna take me to the judge and he'd be real mad at me! Ya know, he [the judge] has knives under his robe and he locks bad kids in a special room with chains and stuff.

Robert was the defendant. He was an experienced child molester who planned his crimes. This was just one of the many ways he tried to frighten his victims into silence. It is not unusual for offenders to give child victims or witnesses seriously misleading information about the legal or community intervention systems that will intimidate or scare them.

Using a model or sketched courtroom is a fun way for children to talk about what they think court will look like, and for the court educator to show the courtroom and explain some of the court processes. Once the court educator has determined that a child does not have unusual fears or misconceptions about court or the judge, the next step is to go on a tour of a real courtroom.

Tour of an Actual Courtroom (and Exits)

When a child has been given the basic information about court, it is time to take him or her on an actual tour of a courtroom. If possible, bring the child to the courtroom in which he or she will be appearing. It is helpful to show a child a courtroom that is not in use, as well as one that is in use.

In an unused courtroom, the child can walk around; examine the surroundings by trying out the microphone and sitting in the various courtroom chairs, including the judge's chair; and even pound the judge's gavel.

Introduce the child to any regular court personnel who happen to be present during the tour. It is okay to introduce a child to a real judge as long as the judge is not going to hear the case in which the witness will appear.

Caution about meeting the judge assigned to the case: Consult with your local prosecutors and defense lawyers about your rules regarding a child witness being introduced to the judge assigned to the case.

Talking with the judge who will hear a particular case, even though the contact is brief and there is no discussion about the case, could be considered an ex-parte communication—a very serious rule violation. If you must ignore a judge who happens to be in a courtroom, inform the child witness that "there is a rule that says we cannot talk with the judge right now. But we can see what (he or she) looks like."

Briefly, show a child a courtroom that is actually being used. Select a courtroom that is handling a matter likely to be mild in tone. Probate and civil court hearings are usually placid and rather safe to view.

Some children want to know where the exits are located in their courtroom. Be sure to show the witness where the exits are located, and especially show the locations of the exits from the witness stand area.

Let the child sit in the witness chair to look around and become familiar with that location. Some witnesses report being worried about someone staring at them when they testify. Show the child some things he or she can look at (visually focus on) when in the courtroom, such as law books, a water pitcher, or a desk corner (that may have a tiny colored sticker on it as a fun reference point).

Closing the Appointment

- Present both the child *and* the parent with your personal business card. The practice of giving a business card to a child demonstrates your respect for him or her. It also serves as a visible link between you and the child.
- Print any special instructions or telephone numbers for the child on the back of the business card, such as "bring your teddy bear," "pack a sandwich," and so on.
- Review with the child any decisions made during the education or preparation meeting, or tasks to be completed, such as the following:
  - ◆ Arrive at noon instead of 10:00 a.m.
  - ◆ Bring in a school picture
  - ◆ Finish Chapter 4 in the workbook
- Remind the parents about any future hearing dates and the purpose of the hearing:
  - ◆ Oct. 10 at 9 a.m.—pretrial (final talk). Room 112
- Review addresses and telephone numbers with the child and parent so that the court educator can stay in touch in the future. Remind parents to inform you about any change of address or telephone number.
- Ask the child if there was anything not talked about or forgotten that should be discussed.
- Remind the child about how to reach you, should he or she think of anything else you should know or should talk about before he or she leaves the building.

Other Common Questions

Subpoenas From the Other Lawyer. Prosecutors and defense lawyers may subpoena the same witnesses for a particular case. What this usually means is that both sides really want to make sure that a particular witness comes to court. It does not matter which side subpoenas a witness to appear in court. Any witness lawfully served with a subpoena is required to honor it and appear in court on the date and time specified.

Sometimes, a victim/witness person or advocate can assist witnesses under dual subpoenas by coordinating with the lawyers involved. After a witness has completed testimony and is excused by the prosecutor, he or she still needs to be excused by the defense lawyer. Usually, when witnesses have completed their testimony in a courtroom, they are done and excused. However, sometimes, one or the other lawyer will want that witness to remain available to be recalled later in the case.

Receiving a subpoena from an opposing lawyer in a case often causes people to think that they did something wrong or are being selected to be on the opposite side. Witnesses should not worry about who issued a subpoena. Receiving a subpoena simply means that a lawyer thinks they may have useful information.

At times, support people or court educators are subpoenaed. Sometimes, these people are legitimate potential witnesses, and other times, this is a tactic or ploy used by the other lawyer to cause confusion or distress, or to exclude the supporter or educator from being in a courtroom with a child.

Immediately inform the case lawyer about any served subpoena that was not anticipated. There may be legal steps that can be taken to remedy this situation if it is a ploy, such as having the support person testify before the child witness, thereby allowing the supporter to be in attendance with the child, or canceling the subpoena completely.

What to Wear to Court. During the closing of the educational process, be sure to let the parents and child know what is considered appropriate and inappropriate attire to wear at the court hearing. Usually, witnesses are asked to wear their nicest conservative clothes. Ask them what they would wear to a special school play, nice family dinner, or church.

Ask parents to share this attire information with anticipated supporters who may be planning to attend a hearing as a spectator. Unknowing spectators sometimes appear for court wearing inappropriate attire and are not admitted into the courtroom. Sharing this wardrobe information with everyone beforehand can prevent problems.

Caps, hats, shorts, t-shirts, short skirts, jeans, tight clothing, low-cut blouses, and tank tops are examples of inappropriate attire. Modest dresses, pump shoes, knee-length skirts, loose blouses, collar shirts, and pressed pants are examples of appropriate attire.

Rules of Sequestration. When they first hear the phrase "witnesses will be sequestered," parents often ask what that means. Sequestration means that witnesses are not permitted to hear or discuss the testimony of another person. Witnesses are sequestered during a trial to ensure that they are not influenced by what they hear and do not alter what they recall about an event. It is very important for supporters, who are listening to testimony in a courtroom, to understand that sequestered witnesses are not permitted to receive information about what is being testified to in the courtroom.

If the child witness takes a recess but has not completed his or her testimony, people who have been inside the courtroom *are not permitted to discuss what has been said in the courtroom* with the child nor to comment on any part of the court proceedings they have viewed.

It is common and natural for support people to want to remark about how a child is testifying, or to comment on what has been said. Because of this natural tendency to want to be nice, and to comment on how a witness is doing, it is imperative that the rules of sequestration be discussed openly with all witnesses and spectators to prevent unwitting violations of this important rule. It is easy to violate a sequestration order, and this can pose significant and serious problems in a case.

Debriefing, Celebrating Efforts, the Verdict, and Sentencing

DEBRIEFING AFTER TESTIMONY IS COMPLETED

When testimony is completed and the child witness is excused from the courtroom, ask the child if he or she wants to talk about the courtroom experience. Ask the child where he or she would like to go to talk. This is an appropriate time to let the child privately vent; share frustrations; and talk about thoughts, perceptions, and emotions. After the child has expressed his or her feelings, begin deescalating and calming the child gradually. Consider doing one of the following:

- Talk or not talk
- Take a walk
- Wait in the waiting room
- Watch a movie in the waiting room
- Go home (if approved by the lawyers)

A hug upon completion of testimony can be quite comforting. Listen to what the child expresses, both good and bad, about the experience. Try to explain, when appropriate, what was going on in court if the child asks a question about something that took place. Permit the child to ask as many questions as desired, and be forthright with your answers.

CELEBRATING THE CHILD'S EFFORTS

Celebrations are suggested as a way to separate the child giving evidence at a civil or criminal trial from the verdict. Avoid having a child equate doing a good job with a particular outcome in the proceedings! If there is an acquittal, or a negative ruling by a judge or jury, a child may conclude that he or she did something wrong. Celebrate the fact that a child tried to do his or her best, no matter what the final outcome may be in a case. Children need to know that testifying truthfully in court is the right thing to do, and that people are proud of them for trying their best.

Children cannot control what happens in a courtroom, nor can they control a verdict decision. Don't wait until a verdict is received in a case to let a child know how proud you are of them for trying their best. If a child finds the courage to go into a courtroom, that effort alone deserves to be recognized—even for children who cannot speak once they get into the witness seat. *Recognize the effort.* Celebrations need not be elaborate. Celebrations can and should be simple and positive. Celebrate the completion of testimony with:

- Hugs
- "High five" hand slaps

- Cupcakes or cookies and milk in the waiting room or at the child's home
- A balloon or sticker

THE VERDICT

There is no way to predict any final outcome in any court matter until the decision is finally reached by a judge or jury. During the court education and preparation process, children and their parents need to be prepared (no matter how strong anyone thinks a case may be) for a verdict of guilty, not guilty, or hung jury. This preparation, although uncomfortable, is really necessary and is a courtesy. It is unkind to not discuss all of the potential outcomes of a case. No one can guarantee a particular verdict in a court case, so all possibilities should be discussed beforehand.

SENTENCING

In criminal cases, if a verdict of guilty is returned by a jury, or the defendant enters a plea, a sentencing hearing will be scheduled. Usually, sentencing hearings are highly emotional, highly charged, and sometimes volatile. Civil, juvenile, dependency, and divorce court final dispositional hearings can be as emotionally charged and difficult as criminal court final hearings. For this reason, children probably should not attend these final court hearings.

However, the final outcome of a criminal sentence or civil disposition hearing should be explained to a child witness in terms he or she would understand. This should be done in a safe and supportive environment.

Presentence Investigative Reports

It is not unusual for a judge to order what is called a *presentence investigative report* (PSI) before passing sentence on a defendant or delinquent. This is a report that is usually done by someone from a community department of corrections or a social service agency. A PSI is an extensive examination of a defendant or delinquent child's history, family background, criminal history, and specifics about the crime. This information is given to the judge before sentencing.

Victim Impact Statements

Many jurisdictions are now including a *victim impact statement* in the PSI. Victim impact statements may be filed separately with judges before sentencing, if they are not included in a formal presentence investigative report.

A victim impact statement is an opportunity for a victim to express to the judge the impact that the crime had on him or her. Crime victims can talk about what happened, if they want, or they can talk about how they feel about being the victim of a crime.

There are some rules about what can be included in a victim impact statement. Feelings about how the crime or event affected a victim; counseling, medical, or restitution issues; and what a victim hopes a sentence may include (but this must be within the legal boundaries fitting the charge) are okay to talk about. Some typical requests that victims want judges to consider imposing on defendants/delinquents are alcohol, drug, or psychological treatment and continued no-contact orders.

Asking for a death sentence for a misdemeanor conviction is an example of an improper consideration request. Similarly, asking a judge to consider imposing a sentence of 20 years for a crime that has a statutory maximum penalty of 5 years would be improper. Appendixes D and E contain sample victim impact statement formats. Appendix D is for child victims, and Appendix E is for the very young child victim.

THANK-YOU LETTERS

Children who testify, or those who are prepared to testify and do not have to do so, should receive an age-appropriate thank-you letter from the case lawyer and/or the court educator if they were willing participants in the court process and wanted to have contact with your agency. Families who were upset with the criminal justice process and indicated that they did not want future contact with anyone within the system should not receive any communication. Be respectful of the various wishes people have.

Simple, brief, and original (not photocopied) thank-you letters should be sent to witnesses. This letter is likely to be the final communication between the lawyer, educator, and child.

Include the following items in a child's thank-you letter:

1. Mention that you are proud of the effort he or she made to talk with you and the judge/jury.
2. Thank the child for trying to do the very best he or she could do.
3. Mention something personal about the child (such as her pet dog, Kippie, or a special article of clothing previously worn).
4. Tell the child that it was nice to meet him or her and wish him or her well in the future.

Dear Kristie:

Thank you very much for testifying in court today. You tried your best, and we are all proud of you. I enjoyed seeing your picture of Kippie. He is a very nice dog.

The picture you drew for me is on the wall in my office. It is a very good picture. I look at it every day.

It was very nice meeting you, and I hope you have a lot of fun swimming this summer.

Your court friend,

Sandy

5

The Court Educator, Lawyer, and Therapist

Most people (adults and children) will indicate that they do not want to go to court to testify. This is a common and expected reaction by most witnesses. Facing the defendant and talking about what happened is one of the most frequently stated reasons for not wanting to testify in court. Fear of making a mistake, or appearing foolish in public, are other common, but less frequently stated reasons that people dread testifying in court. When a child witness expresses or exhibits more than a usual level of fear, anxiety, or stress about facing a defendant in a courtroom, or about going to court in general, the case lawyer should be alerted immediately. It is strongly recommended that the assistance of a mental health professional be sought in these types of cases.

A mental health specialist could offer suggestions and recommendations about how to prepare a traumatized or fearful witness for the courtroom experience. He or she might agree to assist with the preparation process. The lawyer may need to enlist the professional services of a separate mental health professional to assist with determinations about whether a particular witness will be able to testify, or could testify if certain precautions were in place (foundation basis for pretrial motions to modify a courtroom, use closed-circuit television testimony, or use a videotaped deposition of the witness).

Topics discussed in this chapter are as follows:

A. What to look for when screening a case for specialized
   intervention
B. Crisis management vs. therapy
C. The role of a therapist in a court case: What should a therapist ask
   when contacted by a lawyer?
   1. Consultant (not a witness)
   2. An expert witness
   3. Treating therapist
   4. Preparation assistant (possibly becoming a fact witness)
D. Preparation suggestions
   1. Time
   2. Therapy notes
   3. Trauma dolls
   4. Unknown defendant and desensitization
   5. Home visits and office visits

What to Look for When Screening a
Case for Specialized Intervention

The following are examples of some situations or behaviors that should
prompt immediate extra attention and consideration for therapeutic
preparation assistance:

- Child witnesses who verbally express fear about seeing a defendant in court
- Child witnesses who exhibit behaviors such as curling into a fetal
  position, withdrawing, excessive crying, vomiting, or otherwise
  demonstrating difficulty in communicating with a social worker or
  law enforcement officer during the investigative interview
- Child witnesses who are able to talk about many things during the
  educational process, but freeze when they are to talk about what
  happened
- Children who witnessed a violent or explosive situation and are
  fearful about their own safety

- Children who were threatened, confined, or otherwise intimidated during an event
- Cases in which a defendant is known and loved by a family, and there is little or no familial support for the child witness, and the witness will be likely testifying in a manner contrary to the wishes of his or her family
- Children who may have been conditioned by a defendant (see discussion about cuing in Chapter 2)
- Children who appear to dissociate (or are reported to "space out" during the interview)
- Whenever parents tell you that they have great concerns about their child's ability to cope with testifying in court

Crisis Management Versus Therapy

Therapists can help victims and family members work through a myriad of feelings in many ways. Therapeutic assistance, when a case is pending litigation, will likely be in the form of crisis management. Therapy itself may help an individual view a traumatic event differently (known as "reframing"), which might alter the victim's testimony.

When a case is pending litigation and the client is expected to testify at some point in time, the memory of an event is not to be altered. Crisis management is intended to assist the client with finding ways to cope with his or her stress, anxiety, frustration, or worries while waiting for a court case to be resolved without tampering with the client's memory.

The Role of a Therapist in a Court Case: What Should a Therapist Ask When Contacted by a Lawyer?

Find out exactly what will be expected of you. Are you being asked to be a behind-the-scenes consultant to the lawyer, serve as an expert witness, or assist with preparation and crisis intervention services to a particular witness? These roles should be separate, but it is not unusual for lawyers to want to try to blend them. Overlapping or blending roles is not recommended. (Refer to ethical guidelines for psychologists for assistance with this issue.)

CONSULTANT (NOT A WITNESS)

This is the least complicated of requested roles. A therapist in this role serves as a sounding board for the lawyer, who likely wants professional assistance at understanding issues, problems, and dynamics in a case involving a troubled witness. The therapist is an educator for the lawyer and is not going to be called as an expert witness, nor will he or she have to meet with the witness. This eliminates the potential of becoming a fact witness and having to testify.

AN EXPERT WITNESS

Expert witnesses provide knowledge and background to jurors. This is sometimes referred to as a background witness. The primary purpose of expert witness testimony is to educate jurors, so as to help them understand the facts in the particular case on trial before them (Stern, 1997).

Background witnesses provide general scientific background information about basic scientific principles and/or phenomena relevant to a case. They do not express opinions about the specific case. Background witnesses rely on their professional expertise to develop their opinions and usually do not review materials describing the facts of particular cases; such review is unnecessary because these witnesses render opinions about only general scientific issues (Stern, 1997).

TREATING THERAPIST

If a therapist is being asked to assist with seeing a client for the purpose of providing crisis intervention, the therapist should ask the lawyer if he or she is anticipating the need for testimony by the therapist. Even if told no, the therapist should keep and maintain therapy notes in a manner suggested below, for there is no guarantee that the therapist and/or treatment notes will not be subpoenaed later.

Therapists who have not been contacted by a lawyer, but are seeing a witness in therapy who is having difficulty coping with the prospect of testifying, should consider contacting the case lawyer on behalf of the client (with the client's permission). The therapist should ask the lawyer for guidance about any legal conflicts that could occur regarding a contemplated treatment approach to reduce stress and anxiety for the client. The lawyer could advise the therapist about potential forensic problems or difficulties and provide guidance. The therapist could advise the lawyer about ways he or she could work with this witness when going to court.

A therapist discussing with a lawyer some ways to relieve stress or anxiety is not the same as discussing the facts of the case or revealing what has been discussed in confidential therapy sessions. This suggestion is only to help find ways in which the lawyer and therapist can jointly help the client/witness to manage the current situation.

PREPARATION ASSISTANT
(POSSIBLY BECOMING A FACT WITNESS)

A therapist can become a potential fact witness in two ways:

1. *When the therapist is treating a client who becomes involved in a court case.* The therapist could become a potential fact witness in this manner because the client may have revealed certain things during the course of therapy. Therapists in this situation (not knowing that the client would be involved in a court situation when treatment began) are in a difficult position. There could be confidentiality and other issues that could affect their working relationship (in either a positive or negative manner).

2. *When the therapist agrees to assist authorities or a lawyer with a traumatized or troubled witness.* By agreeing to assist in this manner, the therapist is tacitly agreeing to become a fact witness if needed. Becoming a potential fact witness is highly likely for any therapist who agrees to assist with educating or preparing a witness for court. Therapists will be meeting not only with the client in this situation but also with the case lawyer, court educator, and/or victim witness professional.

Preparation Suggestions

TIME

Working with traumatized or very fearful victims or witnesses may require a great investment of time by the court educator, lawyer, and therapist. It is possible that some cases could take days, weeks, or months of time-intensive work by these professionals to adequately prepare some witnesses to testify.

It is important that the case lawyer and therapist spend time together to fully understand each other's roles and expectations. It is also important for the therapist, lawyer, client, and other professionals to spend time together to develop a bond of trust.

THERAPY NOTES

Therapists who see crime victims or witnesses in their practice, or agree to help prepare fearful or traumatized witnesses for court, should learn how to write therapy notes. Some suggestions are as follows:

- Write therapy notes with the expectation that they will be subpoenaed and read in court.
- Write the notes in a manner that can be understood by nontherapists.
- Refrain from writing comments that you would not want printed in a newspaper.
- Use quotation marks around all direct statements made by the client during therapy sessions.
- Discuss confidentiality issues with the client and lawyer before any therapeutic sessions begin. Therapists should let the client know what may be revealed publicly about their sessions. This issue is very complicated and should be thoroughly discussed by the therapist, client, and case lawyer. All parties must be clear about expectations and ramifications of waiving or not waiving confidentiality in each specific situation.

Therapy notes should be detailed, describing the client's demeanor, what is said, and what is asked by the therapist. This can help to combat concerns about leading and suggestive questioning by the therapist. This also assumes that the therapist knows how to ask questions that are not leading and suggestive. Prosecutors and court educators should make sure that local therapists who regularly treat witnesses and crime victims know about this issue.

TRAUMA DOLLS

A representational doll used to therapeutically reduce the trauma of a witness is called a *trauma doll*. The trauma doll is a desensitization tool that is made to depict the person of whom the child is fearful. Some children are extremely afraid of seeing a defendant in the courtroom. When the identity of a defendant is not an issue, and with the approval of the case lawyer, it may be helpful to work with a therapist to start the desensitization process, when appropriate and needed.

The trauma doll is made the same way as a representational doll (previously discussed), except that the representational doll is usually made to look like someone the child likes. Trauma dolls are made to depict someone the child is afraid of.

Supplies Needed to Make a Trauma Doll

1. If a defendant is known by the witness, one or two full face photographs are suggested, with seven copies of each of two photos, or 14 copies of one photo. (Lawyers can request copies of booking photos of defendants from their local law enforcement agency for this purpose.)
2. Cut-out cardboard, construction paper, or wooden people dolls (approximately seven dolls), to be worked on both sides (discussed further)
3. Two 8 x 10 enlargements of any photograph used to make a trauma doll face
4. Color crayons (needed only if the defendant is not previously known, and identity will be an issue in court)
5. Empty shoebox
6. Tape

7. Rubber bands

8. Five to ten rocks that are 1 to 2 inches in size

Making a Trauma Doll

Great care and caution must be exercised by any professional who is working on the issue of reducing a victim's fear of seeing a defendant in the courtroom. Two significant issues need to be discussed—known defendants and unknown defendants. The use of trauma dolls to reduce anxiety and fear levels has been very effective, but it must be stressed that an actual photograph of a defendant *must never be used if the identity of a defendant is in doubt or in question.*

Before using this desensitization technique with a severely traumatized child, the court educator should discuss the issue with a skilled mental health professional (who understands posttraumatic stress symptoms and disorder) and the case lawyer. First, the lawyer must determine whether usage of this tool will pose any problem with court identification. Then, the mental health professional should control the timing and method of introducing the doll to the child.

Trauma dolls or people figures are not much larger than 2 inches high and can be made of plain wood or by drawing a human figure on heavy construction paper and cutting it out. The face of the defendant is cut out of a picture and pasted to the body of the wood or paper figure.

The balance of the body can be left plain, or it can be colored, painted, or decorated by the court educator, therapist, lawyer, or child.

Trauma dolls were originally created for situations in which seeing a previously known perpetrator was absolutely necessary, but all other means of addressing and presenting a traumatized victim's testimony had been exhausted. Desensitization via the trauma doll has been used in cases in which a child clearly knew who the defendant was and was terrified about seeing the defendant in the courtroom.

Children using the trauma doll technique may mutilate or destroy the dolls during the court education and preparation processes. Some children have screamed at the doll, thrown it into walls, or thrown it onto the floor. Other children have taken hammers to the doll, and one child asked his mother to run over it with the car. Accordingly, multiple copies of the doll need to be made in the event that one or more of them are destroyed by the child. Duplicates of the same trauma doll should be distributed to the therapist (three dolls), court educator (two dolls), and lawyer (two dolls). One of the lawyer's dolls is for his or her use during preparation meetings. The other is for admission into evidence, or production in court, should the technique or therapeutic intervention be questioned by opposing counsel, and a doll is needed to show a judge or jury.

Introducing the Trauma Doll to the Child

The trauma doll should be carefully introduced to the child in a supportive environment. The best location is probably at the therapist's office under his or her direct supervision. The witness should be informed about the existence of the doll, and he or she should be allowed to choose whether or not to see the doll. *Never surprise a child with the doll.* If the child does not want to see the doll, the doll should be put away. Ask the child where the doll should be put away, and give him or her the opportunity to choose the location for safekeeping. One option has been to use a shoe box decorated as desired by the child.

With highly traumatized children, the process of seeing the doll typically takes several visits. In these situations, children are frequently willing to work on the shoebox as a place of confinement in lieu of working with the trauma doll itself.

Some children have made shoeboxes into jail cells. Other children have placed small stones inside the box with the doll (to make the doll very uncomfortable). Some children tape the box shut to ensure that the doll remains inside the box, and they readily check on the status of the doll during sessions.

Preparing and decorating the shoebox provides an excellent opportunity for the child to express his or her thoughts about the person in question or the events. This is a safe way for the child to vent and symbolically exercise some control over his or her environment.

Gradually, the doll is brought out of the box, and the child is permitted to do whatever he or she desires with it.

The court educator and lawyer should have duplicate dolls for their use when seeing the child. The mental health professional can use the trauma doll to help assess the child's status, ability, and readiness to enter a courtroom to testify.

After the child gains some mastery over working with the trauma doll, the therapist, court educator, and lawyer may introduce the child to the 8 x 10 photograph.

Some children may tear up the picture. The therapist and court educator should save torn picture pieces in a paper bag for future preparation discussions. Although the photograph is torn, the desensitization process could still continue by using the paper bag (with the torn photograph) as a representation of the defendant.

The key to using a desensitization process with a child is to gradually bring the child closer to the actual courtroom, and to prepare the child to see the defendant in that courtroom.

The issue of the defendant's attendance in the courtroom should be explained to the child in a gentle and slow manner. During this time, it is important for the therapist, court educator, and lawyer to work together at identifying and addressing issues of fear and stress that the child is likely to reveal.

UNKNOWN DEFENDANTS AND DESENSITIZATION

If the defendant in a case is a stranger to the child victim or witness, identification will likely become an issue in court. The steps for preparing the child as stated above should be followed, but with one exception—any hint or suggestion that helps to identify *anyone* must be eliminated. Additional care must be taken during the preparation process to avoid influencing the child's memory of the defendant, or his or her in-court identification of anyone.

One technique for working with a child when a perpetrator was previously unknown, and identity will likely be an issue, is to have the child make a picture or several pictures of the person concerned. When a child draws his or her depiction of what someone looked like—without aid, assistance, or suggestion—the child's own representation can be substituted as the face mentioned above.

All the above techniques can be implemented in the same manner, with the exception of substituting the face of a defendant.

When a defendant was previously unknown to a child witness, and precautions are taken during the education and preparation process, be sure to not indicate where any defendant will be seated when you do your courtroom tour. It is all right to have the trauma doll brought to a courtroom during a tour (to help the child get used to the idea that the defendant may be *somewhere*), but there can be no mention, indication, or confirmation of where any defendant is likely to be seated. Avoid confirming that the person accused of committing a crime will, in fact, be in the courtroom.

One technique that may be used for preparation purposes with a previously unknown defendant is to say, "The police arrested someone for committing this crime, but we don't know if this was the right person. The police sometimes make mistakes. We want to be sure that we have the right person. The person the police arrested may or may not be in the courtroom when you are there. If you see the person who committed the crime, we will want you to tell us that you see him or her. If you don't see the person who committed the crime, we want you to tell us that too, okay?"

HOME VISITS AND OFFICE VISITS

Once a child witness has been deemed to warrant special treatment, he or she should be introduced into the described court process in a slower manner. It may be preferable to have the court educator conduct the initial introductory meeting at this particular child's home, or another location that is more comfortable for the child, such as the therapist's office.

Home visits should take only 5 to 10 minutes, and court should not be discussed with the child. Visits to a therapist's office during a regular session could be brief, or they could last the length of the session. The purpose of a home or therapy session visit is to have the child become personally familiar with the court educator or case lawyer. It will be easier for a traumatized child to go to the courthouse to meet with the court educator or lawyer if they are no longer complete strangers.

During a home visit or therapy session, the court educator or lawyer should approach the child in a gentle and slow manner. Court literature, such as a court-related coloring book or workbook, should be given to the witness (and parent) to work on at their leisure.

Once the child appears less anxious about visiting the court educator's location (this could be after one, two, or more brief home/therapy visits), a court education and preparation schedule may begin. Make appointments with the parents to have the child brought to the court educator's office at times best for the child.

Introduce the issue of court slowly during these initial contact visits. Consider starting a session with a brief play time followed by a brief work session. Gradually talk about what the child has learned about court from the workbook, coloring book, or other literature you gave to the child. Some very traumatized child witnesses have needed approximately 10 to 20 brief educational and/or joint therapy sessions before they were ready to begin the actual preparation process with the lawyer. Each case and child will have different needs and concerns. The amount of time and energy necessary to prepare a child adequately for court will vary, and flexibility will be necessary.

Educating and preparing child victims and witnesses for court can be a difficult yet rewarding experience. The purpose for taking special steps to help a child witness get ready to encounter a court environment is to assist the child witness, in a forensically sound manner, to testify truthfully, accurately, and as completely as possible.

6

A Prosecutor's Perspective on Court Preparation: Boundaries and Roles

Thomas J. Fallon, JD

Topics discussed in this chapter are as follows:

A. The role of the prosecutor
B. Interdisciplinary teamwork
C. Time and effort
D. Vertical versus horizontal case prosecution
E. The charging decision
F. Preliminary hearings and grand juries
G. Preparing the child for court: the prosecutor's responsibility
H. Working with the severely traumatized child
I. Preparing the court for the child: pretrial motion practice
J. Introducing evidence of other acts of abuse
K. The discovery process
L. Videotape and closed-circuit television
M. Contact with the defense: negotiations
N. Meeting with the defense lawyer or investigator
O. Trial considerations and testimonial ties

The Role of the Prosecutor

The prosecutor is the person ultimately responsible for deciding whether someone is going to be charged with a crime, and with what crime. It is not an easy decision. This is especially true when the victim is a child. The decision is also complicated by the fact that the prosecutor is responsible not only to the victim and police but also to the community as a whole. One legal commentator described the complexity of the prosecutor's role as follows:

> The prosecutor . . . enters a courtroom to speak for the People and not just some of the People. The prosecutor speaks not solely for the victim, or the police, or those who support them, but for all the People. That body of "The People" includes the defendant and his family and those who care about him. It also includes the vast majority of citizens who know nothing about a particular case, but who give over to the prosecutor the authority to seek a just result in their name. ("On Prosecutorial Ethics," 1986, pp. 538-539)

Although written years ago, these words assume an even greater meaning for child abuse prosecutors when considered in the context of today's backlash movement. Make no mistake about it, being a prosecutor and doing the job well is no easy task.

In addition to deciding whom should be charged and with what crime, there are other duties that are solely the responsibility of the prosecutor, such as the following:

- Deciding when to issue the charge(s)
- Presenting evidence at the preliminary hearing or grand jury
- Preparing the child to testify in court
- Preparing the court for the child
- Filing other crimes and bad acts motions, which may involve the testimony of other victims
- Exchanging information with the defense prior to trial (i.e., the discovery process)
- Deciding whether to videotape or use closed-circuit televised testimony (CCTV)
- Negotiating a plea with the defense
- Developing a trial strategy
- Meeting with the defense lawyer or investigator
- Presenting the case at trial and disposition

The duties and responsibilities of prosecutors are as extensive as their influence. However, that influence has its limits. In child abuse cases, prosecutors sometimes overestimate the importance of their role. First, they fail to recognize that the abuse upon which the criminal case is premised occurred before, often long before, the prosecutor became involved. Second, they fail to appreciate that the effects of the abuse and the systemic response to that abuse, of which the prosecutor is a big part, will linger long after the prosecutor has moved on to the next case.

Interdisciplinary Teamwork

Child abuse often means the interaction of some or all of the following disciplines:

- Mental health
- Child development
- Linguistics
- Social services
- Medicine
- Law enforcement
- Education
- Law

Any response requiring court intervention must have the interaction of all of the disciplines involved in a given case. An interdisciplinary *team* approach is the best way to accomplish a community's coordinated response.

For prosecutors, this means that they must acquire a working knowledge of the medical and social sciences to be successful. For example, familiarity with the research on children's memory, suggestibility, and linguistic capabilities is critical in assessing whether a child abuse disclosure is the product of an impermissibly suggestive forensic interview. Because none of this is taught in law school, it must be learned on the job and at interdisciplinary training conferences. Many new ideas and innovative courtroom techniques used today have their origins in the research done by social workers, psychologists, and therapists.

Interdisciplinary team members are excellent resources for ideas as well as expert testimony. Any information that leads to a greater understanding of the complexities of child abuse and its effects on human behavior enhances the prosecutor's ability to use the law to achieve a truly fair and just result in court. Similarly, a well-informed prosecutor can use his or her knowledge of the social sciences to direct and shape investigative efforts and procedures. This, in turn, will result in the development of more accurate and forensically reliable information that will be useful to all team members, not just the prosecutor.

Some of the more indispensable interdisciplinary team members are those who help the prosecutor prepare the child for court. These victim/ witness professionals or court educators provide a myriad of services, ranging from establishing communication links with other disciplines to counseling victims and their families about the vagaries and complexities of the criminal justice system. They act as both buffer and bridge between prosecutor and victim.

In addition, they may be in a position to offer testimony in the courtroom for a variety of purposes. Courts may permit these professionals to render "advice to the judge when appropriate and as a friend of the court, regarding the child's ability to understand proceeding and questions" (Wisconsin Statute 950.055(2)). These professionals may also provide assistance in making determinations concerning the taking of videotape depositions and the duty to expedite court proceedings (Wisconsin Statute 971.105).

Finally, an interdisciplinary response leads to the sharing of ideas and information among the disciplines. That, in turn, will lead to a more child-centered systemic response; the development of more accurate and reliable information regarding the child involved; and a greater understanding of the constellation of legal, social, and psychological issues present in each and every child abuse case. From this sharing of ideas and information, better decision making results, which increases the likelihood of a just and fair outcome in court and an improved mental health outlook for the child.

Time and Effort

Family violence in general, and child abuse cases in particular, routinely consume large amounts of time. They truly test one's patience and stamina. The degree of success experienced in these cases is directly related to the amount of time and effort invested, more so than just about any other case. Because these cases are so time-consuming, successful prosecutors often contribute much of their own time and energy. Prosecutors meet with the child and his or her family when it is convenient for the child and not the prosecutor. This means long hours and weekends of work.

Prosecutors must assess the child's credibility, ability to communicate, and emotional readiness for court before bringing a case to court. In special cases, a prosecutor may need to meet with the child several times before charging the case. These meetings may include the court educator or victim/witness specialist, especially if the prosecutor intends to discuss the abuse scenario with the child. It is important that the prosecutor is not the sole witness to something the child says or does, which could be considered inculpatory or exculpatory evidence.

Some of the cases that routinely consume vast amounts of time before a charging decision can be made are cases where

- the child has been victimized by more than one perpetrator, or there are numerous child victims, as in day care cases;
- the child is developmentally delayed and/or impaired;
- there are repeated acts of intrafamilial abuse;
- the child is severely traumatized as a result of the abuse;
- force or the threat of force was used to keep the child silent or was inflicted during the abuse.

Often, more than one of these factors is present. In such cases, prosecutors need more time to establish rapport and the ability to communicate with the child. Many prosecutors make the mistake of confusing the ability to establish rapport with the ability to communicate effectively with the child. It is not unusual for a prosecutor to establish a wonderful surface rapport with a child, only to have things fall apart in the courtroom because there was a failure to communicate. There was a failure to understand the distinction between getting along in one setting and real communication in court. It is imperative that the prosecutor and the child establish a level of trust and find the means to communicate effectively with each other. If not, the case will surely be lost, and the child may experience additional trauma as a result of this failure.

In cases where there are allegations of extensive and repetitive intrafamilial abuse, multiple offenders, or severe trauma, prosecutors and other members of the interdisciplinary team must spend time with the child before charges are filed. These time investments help the prosecutor screen out cases that ordinarily would have been issued prematurely, with disastrous consequences. Time investment has also helped to successfully present other cases because a trusting relationship developed with the child over a period of time that enabled the child to communicate and emotionally handle the rigors of the adversarial system.

Vertical Versus Horizontal Case Prosecution

One of the best ways to improve the handling of child abuse cases and their presentation in court is to implement a vertical case prosecution system.

Vertical case prosecution requires that the same prosecutor who initially screens the case and makes the charging decision also handles the case throughout the court process, from the first appearance in court through disposition. This does not occur in offices that have a horizonal case prosecution system.

Horizontal case prosecution involves a rotating caseload. This means that different prosecutors may handle the charging decision, initial appearance, probable cause hearing, arraignment, pretrial motion work, trial, and dispositional hearing. This happens because cases are randomly assigned from court to court. The defense may request a substitution of a judge, thus removing the case from the court where a prosecutor familiar with the case is assigned to another court with a prosecutor who is not. Perhaps there is insufficient staffing (this is one of the most common reasons) to permit each prosecutor to follow a given case and handle each and every aspect of this case.

Many prosecutors' offices do not have the staffing or the cooperation of the judiciary to implement a complete vertical case prosecution system. There are, of course, exceptions. Historically, homicides and cases generating extensive public interest (e.g., public corruption or organized crime) are often handled by the same prosecutor from beginning to end. Clearly, vertical case prosecution is the preferred method for handling all criminal cases. However, because most prosecutors' offices face significant personnel shortages, it is difficult, if not impossible, to have one prosecutor handle every aspect of each case from beginning to end. Nevertheless, some sort of vertical prosecution must be achieved in sensitive crime cases, such as domestic violence and child abuse. This is especially true because these cases often involve child victims and witnesses. If the vertical case prosecution system is used in homicides, organized crime, public corruption, and other high-profile public interest cases, it can and should be used in child abuse cases as well.

One solution is to have the attorney who screens the case and makes the charging decision be responsible for all critical aspects of the case. For example, it may not be necessary for this prosecutor to appear at the initial appearance or bail proceeding, because these are often perfunctory in nature and can be handled by other prosecutors with a limited amount of direction and guidance. However, other aspects, such as meeting the child, preparing the child for court, and court appearances that involve the taking of testimony, should all be handled by the same prosecutor.

Another approach is to establish specialized units that work exclusively with these types of cases, with at least one prosecutor assigned to each and every branch of court that handles child abuse cases.

A third approach is a slight variation of the second. Designate a sufficient number of specialized prosecutors to handle all of these cases, and assign other cases to them as needed. Vertical prosecution can ensure that only experienced and trained prosecutors are handling these cases.

Vertical handling of cases is the best system for developing expertise. Vertical prosecutions improve the handling of cases from both an administrative and a legal perspective. Moreover, the public's opinion regarding the competency and professionalism of the office will improve. Finally, vertical prosecutions generally provide the prosecutor with more time to devote to the preparation of the witnesses and the case in general than do horizontal prosecutions. They permit more time for regular communication with the child's court educator or victim/witness professional, and for the development of rapport and the ability to communicate effectively with the child victim in court.

The Charging Decision

The decision to charge a person with a crime remains the greatest exercise of prosecutorial discretion. The decision to prosecute or not to prosecute carries far-reaching and long-lasting implications for victim and offender alike. Of equal importance to the decision to charge someone with a crime are the decisions regarding when and in what manner the charges should be issued (i.e., arrest without warrant, arrest with warrant, or by summons).

Although ethical considerations permit prosecutors to issue charges once probable cause exists, most prosecutors issue charges only if they are convinced that they can prove their case beyond a reasonable doubt. Usually, prosecutors refrain from issuing charges until the investigation is complete or nearly complete, and reasonable alternative hypotheses have been explored and ruled out. There are, however, exceptions.

First, if the child victim is in danger of repeated abuse from a delay to complete the investigation, then the charging decision probably will be expedited. Similarly, if delay puts other children at risk, then the prosecutor is more likely to issue charges quickly as long as there is probable cause to believe that the crime has occurred and that the investigation can be completed within a reasonable time.

Second, if there is a reasonable belief that the offender will flee, prosecutors will consider expediting the charges, even though the investigation is not complete, if they have probable cause to arrest and likewise believe that the investigation can be completed in a short time.

Third, if the prosecutor has a reasonable belief that evidence will disappear or be destroyed, he or she may issue charges to prevent this.

Closely related to the decision of when to issue charges is the decision of how the charge should be issued. Equally challenging is the decision to begin a prosecution with an arrest without a warrant, an arrest with a warrant, or a summons. Many of the considerations overlap with those involved in timing the commencement of the prosecution. Although each case is unique, there are a number of inquiries that are common to all cases.

The following is an illustrative, but by no means exclusive, list of questions that a prosecutor might ask in deciding how a case should begin:

- Is the investigation complete? If not, how long will it take to wrap it up?
- Is the offender aware that the crime has been reported or that he or she is being investigated?
- Is it likely the offender will flee the jurisdiction?
- Is it likely the offender will take steps to destroy or hide critical evidence?
- Is the child victim, or other children, at risk for continued abuse while attempts are made to complete the investigation?
- If the case is one of intrafamilial abuse, will the nonoffending parent be supportive of the child? If not, is the child likely to recant under pressure from the nonoffending parent or siblings?

Again, much like the timing consideration, if it appears that the suspect will flee, evidence will disappear, or a child is at risk, an immediate arrest, with or without a warrant, is a likely choice. However, in other situations, where the child is not at risk for immediate future harm or the offender is unaware of the investigation, it is likely that the prosecutor will take the time to complete the investigation before commencing the prosecution. Depending on the severity of the offense and the defendant's stature in the community (i.e., the likelihood that the offender would flee and post bail in any event), the prosecution may be commenced upon a warrant or a summons.

Prosecutors continuously evaluate whether more will be gained or lost by proceeding quickly with an arrest as opposed to taking the time to be as thorough as possible in putting their case together. Essentially, it is a complex cost-benefit analysis with many human variables; in fact, so many human variables that it is almost impossible to determine the right course of action in every case. It is usually in the best interest of the child and the prosecution to proceed as quickly as possible, but there are always some cases that demand a slower pace. For example, in cases involving very young children, it may be better to proceed more slowly. The additional time allows the child to gain valuable communication skills. For some children, the additional time and ensuing preparation will help them become emotionally ready for court. The down side, of course, may be a loss of memory from too long of a delay.

Even though the decision to prosecute, as well as when and how the prosecution should commence, is solely that of the prosecutors, it should be an informed decision, one that includes input from members of the interdisciplinary team involved with that child (unless, for some reason, the investigation requires complete confidentiality, but this is rare). These members will almost always include law enforcement, social service, and victim/witness representatives. However, other members of the interdisciplinary team, such as the therapist, physician, or special education teacher may have valuable information that will assist the prosecutor in making a more informed decision.

The interdisciplinary team and court educator can provide valuable information to the prosecutor, thus helping him or her make a more informed charging decision. For example, they can provide information on the family dynamics in a particular case at hand; the nonoffending caregiver's attitude toward the child; or the strengths, weaknesses, or special needs of the child victim/witness.

Because every case has a life and a pace all its own, timing is everything. Thus, armed with information from the team, the prosecutor can decide to do one of the following:

- Stay the present course because there is no need to alter the investigation or preparation pace.
- Speed up and expedite issuing the charge.
- Slow down and delay issuing charges until adequate time has been spent investigating the case and working with the child.
- Stop or suspend the process indefinitely.

It is possible that some children will never be able to provide information to support a charge or to testify in court under any circumstances. In these cases, the decision not to issue criminal charges, although difficult, is the correct decision. It is at this point that one should explore other options, such as a child protection proceeding in juvenile court or a modification of the visitation or custody order, if one exists. Finally, if court intervention is simply not possible, it does not mean that we simply forget about the child or the family. Some other community response must occur, perhaps from the Department of Social Services, a therapist, or a community support group.

Preliminary Hearings and Grand Juries

Some states have preliminary hearings; others have grand juries; and some states, such as Washington, have neither. Preliminary and grand jury hearings are proceedings that are held to establish probable cause to believe that a crime occurred and that the person arrested or charged with the crime probably committed it. If probable cause is established, further proceedings are merited. If probable cause is not found, the charge will be dismissed.

Prosecutors decide whether a child must or should testify in these preliminary proceedings. Crime victims often testify in these proceedings, but this is not always the case when the victim is a child. There are some legal exceptions that permit prosecutors to continue the prosecution without having the child victim testify at the preliminary hearing or grand jury. Nevertheless, there are situations in which a child must testify because there is no legal alternative. This happens more often in states with a preliminary hearing system. In states using the preliminary hearing, the offender is present at the hearing, and the child is subject to cross-examination. The public is usually permitted to attend as well.

On the other hand, children rarely, if ever, testify before a grand jury. Offenders are not present at grand juries, nor are most of these proceedings open to the public. Although children rarely testify in the grand jury system, they still must testify at trial. Consequently, they need every bit as much, if not more, preparation for trial as those children who have testified at the preliminary hearing.

There are risks in having a child testify at a preliminary hearing. Some of those risks are as follows:

- The child freezes on the witness stand and is unable to speak (i.e., the child experiences more trauma).
- The child makes inconsistent statements, or the child recants his or her statements.
- The child is not a good witness, thus making the case more difficult to negotiate and less likely to go to trial.
- The child may be subjected to extensive and numbing cross-examination by defense counsel, which may be entirely counter-productive to the child's mental health and the case in general.

There are also benefits to having children testify at preliminary hearings, assuming, of course, that they are well prepared. Some of those benefits are as follows:

- Such testimony affords an opportunity for a child to practice testifying in court without a courtroom filled with people (yes, some people will be present, but generally, preliminary hearings do not generate the public interest that trials do). The child also gets used to testifying in the presence of the defendant. This experience can strengthen the child's confidence and empower him or her to testify at trial.
- It provides an opportunity to assess the child's linguistic and cognitive abilities, as well as the child's credibility under fire.
- The preliminary hearing testimony may yield information that supports additional charges, or that the current charge be amended or dismissed, all of which may increase the chances for a successful prosecution or a significant savings of time and emotional stress.
- Children who testify in these preliminary proceedings will have an opportunity to talk with the prosecutor, court educator, or victim/witness professional about their experience. The prosecutor and the court educator or victim/witness professional will have a good idea of what can be done to improve as they prepare for trial.
- The issues are limited and the burden of proof low enough that the risks discussed above are minimized as the child and prosecutor gain valuable experience working together. It is a good time to test one's ability to communicate in the heat of battle.

- A properly prepared child who testifies well at a preliminary hearing increases the prosecutor's ability to negotiate a favorable resolution to the case. A prosecutor negotiates from a position of strength rather than weakness. Well-investigated cases with properly prepared child witnesses are resolved with plea agreements without the necessity of a trial. Even if you cannot resolve the case, the time spent preparing the child for the preliminary hearing provides a solid foundation upon which trial preparation will occur.

Some prosecutors look at preliminary hearings as "speed bumps" or road blocks on the way to trial. But the adversarial nature of a preliminary hearing provides a proving ground to try out new ideas and strategies. It may be a good opportunity to "test the waters" with novel motions to do the following:

- Modify the courtroom to make the child more comfortable by providing age-appropriate furniture for the child
- Request that age-appropriate language and grammar be used when questioning the child regardless of whether the examiner is a prosecutor or defense attorney
- Try out certain techniques that may affect the accused's Sixth Amendment right to confrontation, such as the use of blackboards, screens, closed-circuit television, or videotape (discussed in greater detail later in the chapter).

There are many prosecutors who have had success in trial and in plea negotiations in jurisdictions where the child does not testify at a preliminary proceeding, choosing instead to establish their proofs through other witnesses. If you are successful in your outcomes with your current strategy of using child witness testimony at these preliminary proceedings, then you probably shouldn't change. However, if you are looking for ways to improve, you might want to think about having the child testify in preliminary proceedings.

In any event, the decision to use live child victim testimony at these preliminary proceedings may be entirely dependent on the philosophical predilections of the magistrates, commissioners, and judges who handle these proceedings. There are many judicial officers who construe the rules of evidence so strictly that it is virtually impossible to obtain a probable cause finding without testimony from the child.

Similarly, many magistrates do not permit the creation of a child-friendly environment. They do not permit modifications to the courtroom, limiting the length of the testimony, or controlling the mode of examination. The prosecutor must consider all of these realities on a case-by-case basis in making the decision and continue to do what works best in his or her jurisdiction.

Preparing the Child for Court:
The Prosecutor's Responsibility

The job of preparing the child to testify in court, although shared with other professionals, is primarily the responsibility of the prosecutor. The prosecutor should not delegate this responsibility (i.e., testimonial preparation) to a victim/witness specialist, court educator, or any other professional without first providing that person with appropriate training and supervision.

The prosecutor should meet with the child's court educator or victim/witness professional before meeting with the child. Ideally, the court educator or victim/witness professional will introduce the prosecutor to the child once the basic court education and preparation course has been completed, unless the prosecutor met with the child during the precharging or screening process.

The court educator or victim/witness professional should be able to describe and explain the child's emotional condition and developmental abilities—how well the child comprehended and answered questions during the preparatory functions, and any unusual, special, or problematic issues discovered during their time together.

Support personnel should be assigned the responsibility of helping to create an atmosphere conducive to obtaining truthful and accurate testimony from the child in court, whereas a prosecutor is responsible for preparing the presentation of the testimony.

There are a number of other things that prosecutors should keep in mind when handling these cases. First, have another person present to act as a witness whenever you are discussing the particulars of the abuse with the child in order to avoid the possibility of the prosecutor becoming the sole witness to inculpatory or exculpatory information.

Consider using a victim/witness professional, law enforcement officer, or other professional. Using the court educator or victim/witness professional may be convenient if either has established a trusting relationship with the child and the police investigator is unable to attend. However, there is always the risk that this person may become a witness and be unable to continue functioning as support personnel due to the rules of witness exclusion or sequestration, as discussed earlier in this book.

Second, avoid meeting the child for the first time on the day you are going to court to elicit testimony. Some children may need only one visit to establish a communication bond before going to court to testify. Other children may need two, three, or four meetings with the prosecutor before they are ready to testify.

Preparation should begin as soon as possible. Some cases may require a child's testimony within days of the offender's arrest. Therefore, the prosecutor may have to arrive early and stay late or alter personal plans to accommodate as many meetings as necessary in a given case.

Third, be sincere with the child, and do not rush the child. Do not force a discussion of substantive issues if the child is not ready. It is better to use the time to continue building rapport and demonstrate that the child's wishes will be respected when possible. Generally, you can come back on another day to discuss substantive matters such as the abuse scenario. The more time you spend with the child, the more likely you will recognize when the child is ready to talk.

Fourth, be respectful of the child in both word and deed. One of the best ways to respect the child is to respect the child's sense of space. Do not touch a child until the child indicates a willingness to be touched. Do not approach the child in a threatening way. Let the child come to you.

Fifth, do not make promises you cannot keep. For example, promising a child that his or her mother will be allowed to sit with him or her when testifying is risky. This decision is the judge's and the judge's alone. For whatever reason, a judge may not permit that accommodation.

Do not promise a child that he or she will be done testifying on a particular day and will never have to talk about "it" again. Too many things can go wrong to make this statement. There may be a mistrial or continuance, the defense may wish to recall the child later in the case, or the case could be reversed on appeal and a new trial ordered. Thus, your statement to the child would not be truthful, and any trust developed between you and the child might be lost.

Sixth, learn to recognize the signs of trauma and/or stress in the child. The prosecutor should spend time listening to and observing the child's behaviors as he or she reacts to questioning by others. Note when a child pauses, hesitates, or demonstrates some discomfort. Talk with the child about what he or she is thinking and feeling. Discuss openly and honestly why you need to probe these uncomfortable subjects. Talk about ways in which the child can tell you when he or she needs to take a break or change topics. This ability to communicate with children and recognize stress is critical in the courtroom when a child begins to experience difficulty on the witness stand.

Seventh, in difficult cases, ask a mental health professional for assistance as you prepare the child for court. (See discussion below for more detail.)

Eighth, learn the child's developmental capabilities, and practice communicating with the child so that you can talk with the child on his or her level. The only way a prosecutor will recognize trouble signs is to meet with the child personally and talk with him or her at some length. Each child is different.

It is important to note that more time is probably spent on developing rapport and communication skills than on the particulars of the abuse scenario. Some suggested topics to discuss are as follows:

- General family information
- School
- Sporting events
- What it's like to be a witness
- The court process in general
- Pets
- Outside interests

The list is almost endless. Do not be afraid to talk with the child about your role in the process, and take time to explain to the child the roles of the other people the child will meet during the process. Talk with the child about what is expected of him or her. It is important to give the child instructions to help him or her handle questioning in court.

Some examples of sample instructions are as follows:

- "Your job is to listen to the questions and tell us what really happened."
- "Talk out loud so that everyone can hear you."
- "If someone says something that is wrong, please tell us that it is wrong." The child should be told that sometimes adults make mistakes, and that we want the child to tell us if any mistakes are made.
- "It is OK to say 'I don't know.' " It is critical to tell the child that he or she doesn't have to know all of the answers.

Working With the Severely Traumatized Child

In cases where the child is severely traumatized, it is advisable to consult with the child's counselor or therapist, if he or she has one, or with a therapist from your interdisciplinary team if he or she does not. It might be advisable to hire a therapist for the important, but limited, task of caring for the child's emotional health during the stress of preparing for and testifying in court. Some examples of behaviors that should prompt you to ask for help from a mental health professional are as follows:

- The child dissociates (appears not to hear you; fails to respond to cues or talk; does not respond to his or her given name and/or refers to him- or herself by another name; informs you he or she is "gone"; fails to recall meeting or talking with you before, when, in fact, you have talked before).
- The child coils into a fetal position when you begin to talk to him or her about difficult topics, such as the abuse scenario.
- The child cries and appears terribly distressed (this is different from a witness who is scared and hesitant, but able to communicate his or her thoughts and feelings).

- The child mentions or makes a gesture of suicide, or wanting to commit a violent act.
- The child self-mutilates.
- The child breathes rapidly or has difficulty breathing; the child sweats or vomits.
- The child rocks steadily in a seated position and fails to respond to verbal or physical cues.

If any of these behaviors are observed and reported to the prosecutor, it is time to slow down, reevaluate, and seek help from the mental health professional.

The case described below is one in which the prosecutors benefited significantly from working with a clinical psychologist.

> Two sisters were severely abused by their father and stepfather. The youngest child was 6½ years of age but functioned at the level of a 3½- to 4-year-old. It was very difficult to prepare the younger child for trial. The child would not talk about the abuse except when she was shown photographs of her battered and bruised buttocks. These injuries were the precipitating factor that brought the child to the attention of the local authorities. When the photographs were shown to the child, she became very emotional, tearful, and terribly stressed. This made the prosecutors very uncomfortable.

Because the trauma experienced by this child was so significant, funding arrangements were made through the State Department of Justice, Office of Crime Victim Assistance program. This enabled the prosecutors to retain a psychologist specifically to assist them in preparing the child for court without unnecessarily traumatizing her further.

The psychologist helped the prosecutors understand posttraumatic stress disorder and how it affected the child. Together, they explored the limits of how far they could go in having the child reexperience the abuse so that she could talk and then testify about the abuse. With the help of the psychologist, the prosecutors were able to communicate with the child on her level and earn her trust so that she was able to testify at trial with only a minimal amount of trauma. She did, in fact, testify—not once, not twice, but actually four times! She testified at two preliminary hearings and two jury trials. Both of her abusers were convicted, and she and her sister were able to be placed in a safe and secure environment.

All of the professionals involved in the case, including the police, social workers, therapists, and prosecutors, believe that the trials and all of the preparation associated with them were not harmful to her.

In difficult cases, conducting this type of preparation with the assistance of a highly skilled therapist is a rewarding experience, highly recommended, and necessary if the offenders who perpetrate such trauma are ever going to be held accountable.

Preparing the Court for the Child: Pretrial Motion Practice

The first five chapters of this book and the preceding section of this chapter have focused on preparing the child for court. This section focuses on preparing the court for the child's testimony. It is simply the other side of the same coin. Sadly, it is an aspect of child abuse case preparation that is overlooked.

Pretrial motions are formal, usually written, legal requests made by lawyers to judges asking that something happen or not happen during the trial or at some other court proceeding. Too often, prosecutors find themselves on the defensive, responding to a multitude of motions brought by the defense. Examples include motions to

- Suppress statements
- Suppress identification
- Discover information
- Adjourn or continue the proceedings to another date
- Substitute judges
- Change venue
- Suppress the child's statement because the child's statements resulted from an impermissibly suggestive forensic interview. These suppression hearings are often called "taint" hearings. Essentially, it is argued that the information obtained from the child is unreliable; moreover, the child's memory has been affected by the impermissibly suggestive interview tactics such that the expected

courtroom testimony is untrustworthy. Therefore, it should not be heard by the jury.

Similarly, prosecutors should file motions that facilitate obtaining accurate and reliable testimony from children (i.e., motions that aid the truth-finding function of the court). After all, the jury trial is a search for the truth. Prosecutors should consider filing motions of their own to balance the scales in the courtroom and level the playing field for the children. Examples of such pretrial motions are requests to

- dispense with asking very young children to give an oath. A simple promise to tell what really happened is legally sufficient (*State v. Hanson,* 1989).
- dispense with competency determinations by the court, as well as trick questions, such as, "What is the difference between a truth and a lie?" Most witnesses, especially in states that have adopted a version of the Federal Rules of Evidence, are presumed competent (*State v. Hanson,* 1989).

  Children as young as 3 years of age can be competent to testify, but a child must be able to understand the questions and articulate an answer. In order for the child to qualify as a witness, you must show that the child understands his or her obligation to tell the truth and knows that some earthly consequence can befall him or her for lying. This is not to suggest, however, that a child must be incredibly bright. An average child, less than 6 years of age, with good verbal skills, is often a competent and successful witness, even though the child may tend to digress upon occasion (Smith, 1985).
- schedule a particular time of day for the child's testimony (Cal. Penal Code Sec. 868.8, 1989).
- schedule multiple recesses based upon the limited attention span that young children have.
- change spatial arrangements in the courtroom to allow the child to sit at a more child-friendly table or chair.
- simplify vocabulary and sentence structure used in the questioning of children to avoid the use of the following:
  - ◆ the passive voice
  - ◆ pronouns

- ◆ relational concepts
- ◆ double negatives
- ◆ a "Do you remember x?" question
- ◆ an "Isn't it true that . . . ?" question
- ◆ adult vocabulary
- Leading and suggestive questions on cross-examination. If they are so dangerous and so unfair in the investigative process, then the defense should be precluded from using leading and suggestive questions on cross-examination.
- permit support persons to be present in the courtroom during the child's testimony.
- permit the child to sit on the lap of a support person during testimony.
- use videotape, screens, or closed-circuit television.
- use other acts evidence (discussed in greater detail below).
- expedite the proceedings (see Wisconsin Statute 971.105).
- use or preclude expert witness testimony.

The arguments made in favor of these motions should not be based solely on the assertion that they will reduce trauma, even though this is probably true. The real reason, and more important reason, for these requests is that they will, indeed, facilitate the search for the truth by obtaining more reliable and accurate information from the child.

The literature is now replete with research that children provide more accurate information when they are asked direct, simple, and focused questions (for a summary of this research, see Myers, Goodman, & Saywitz, 1996). Children who are cross-examined with adult language in harsh voices, as is often the case in our courts, do not provide as much accurate information as those examinations that are done in a child-focused way.

Courts are required by law to provide accommodations to all members of our society who are mentally and physically challenged pursuant to the Americans with Disabilities Act (ADA) so that they will have access to our courts. For years, courts have provided interpreters to sign for deaf witnesses and defendants. We should afford these same considerations to our children. It is not fair to expect a child to come to court and communicate using adult language, behaviors, and mannerisms. A child can communicate only on a child's level. We cannot expect children to do something that they are, by their very nature, incapable of doing. Unfortunately, this occurs in our courts every day.

Because prosecutors are responsible for bringing these cases to court, they should make every effort to ensure that the children are treated with as much dignity and respect as adult victims. Support for granting these motions is found in the research literature and in the statutory rules of evidence, as noted in Federal Rule of Evidence 611:

611. Mode and order of interrogation and presentation.

(1) CONTROL BY JUDGE. The judge shall exercise reasonable control over the mode and order of interrogating witnesses and presenting evidence so as to:
   a) Make the interrogation and presentation effective for the ascertainment of the truth,
   b) avoid needless consumption of time, and
   c) protect witnesses from harassment or undue embarrassment.

Thus, the decision to grant such a motion rests in the sound discretion of the trial court. Examples of such a motion with supporting memorandum are provided in Appendixes G and H.

Introducing Evidence of Other Acts of Abuse

One of the signs of a comprehensive and complete investigation is the documented effort to locate other victims. All prior police contact reports involving an offender should be read carefully to determine the true nature and extent of the reported incident. If significant effort is made to find other victims, or find that the offender engaged in other bad acts that may be relevant to an issue at hand, the chances are much greater that the case will be resolved with a plea to the appropriate charge or charges. That means that the children will be spared the ordeal of testifying in court.

If other victims are located, the prosecutor should seek to admit their testimony. This testimony is extremely powerful. Once the court decides to admit such testimony, the chances of a plea, or conviction after trial, improve substantially.

One of the things that a prosecutor can do to increase his or her chances of filing a motion is to request that investigative officers and child protective workers never end a forensic interview without asking this question: "Do you know if this happened to anyone else?" The chances are pretty good that the child will answer "yes." Even though this question and answer, by their very nature, will result in a significant amount of additional work, the benefits are well worth the time and effort.

The Discovery Process

Discovery is a legal term for requesting information from the opposing party that is relevant to the case at hand. It is regulated by statute. Every state permits some form of discovery. Prosecutors should attempt to discover as much about the defense case as possible. Thus, another pretrial motion worthy of discussion is a motion for reciprocal discovery.

Disclosure of information should be a two-way street. Some of the more important pretrial discovery requests involve the following:

- Discovering the identity of expert witnesses to be employed by the defense
- Discovering the nature of the anticipated testimony of the defense expert
- Obtaining copies of their reports and the information upon which their opinions are based
- Obtaining any scientific, psychological, or psychiatric testing done on behalf of the accused

Videotape and Closed-Circuit Television

Some jurisdictions videotape the forensic interviews of child victims and use this tape to supplement live testimony. Other jurisdictions use videotaped depositions, which are examinations under oath in the presence of the offender that are then presented in court in lieu of live testimony. Closed-circuit television is another means by which a child testifies in court but from a different location. The child's testimony is heard and viewed on a television screen. Comments here will be limited to the use of videotape in the presentation of the state's case, whether in the form of investigative interviews, depositions, or closed-circuit television.

Much has been said and written about the pros and cons of videotaped investigative interviews that need not be repeated here. Much the same can be said for videotaped depositions and closed-circuit television. The use of videotape is a hotly debated issue in child abuse cases (Stephenson & Stern, 1992).

There are many prosecutors who refuse to use videotape or closed-circuit television even though their statutes permit it. On the other hand, there are many other prosecutors who swear by these techniques and use them with great success. The advice in this segment is simple: If you use videotape in your jurisdiction, and you are successful in the results you obtain at trial and in the way you treat child victims and their families, do not change. If you are successful without the use of videotape, don't change. The old adage "if it ain't broke, don't fix it" applies here.

However, if you are undecided as to whether you should use videotape or closed-circuit testimony, there are some issues to consider. First, what are the child's feelings with respect to the use of videotape? A child should be told that he or she is going to be videotaped, regardless of whether it is a forensic interview or deposition. The child's feelings should be given due consideration by prosecutors and investigators.

Many people underestimate children and assume that a child will not want to testify in court. Other people assume that a child will be harmed by testifying in court. However, most children, even some who are severely traumatized, are able to testify in court without lingering adverse effects when they are prepared properly.

Proper preparation by all involved concerning a child's testimony is the key to success for making the courtroom experience one that is at least a neutral, if not positive, experience for the child. On the other hand, there are some children who will not be able to testify in court for a variety of reasons, and an alternative, such as videotape, should be explored.

Second, and this may be contrary to conventional wisdom, juries want to see and believe children in court. Moreover, many prosecutors would rather have a live witness on the stand and will do everything that is both legal and ethical to prepare the child for that experience.

Furthermore, the potential exists for sending the wrong message to a jury if we create too many specialized procedures that facilitate getting the child's story across without the child being present. We run the risk of sending a message to the jury in particular, and society in general, that children are second-class citizens who are incapable of providing truthful, accurate, and credible testimony, even though a sizable amount of social science research indicates to the contrary.

Children can and do provide accurate testimony just like adults. Children should have access to our courts and should be heard in court just like adults. We spent the past 45 years ensuring that our courts are open to all of our citizens regardless of race, color, creed, ethnicity, or disability. The courts exist for everyone, and we should do our best to allow our children to participate in person, just as we do for any other member of society. Therefore, before we embrace the use of videotape, closed-circuit television, or any other special procedure, we must be aware of the effects that their use has on society, and we must be cautious and realistic in what we expect from it.

Third, if either videotaped depositions or closed-circuit television is to be employed, we must first realize that these techniques require the same amount of preparation as live testimony. Additional time and work will be required to make sure that the legal foundation upon which the court can safely render a decision permitting the use of videotape, and that will be upheld on appeal, is solid. This is especially true if one is relying on the argument that live testimony will be too emotionally harmful to the child witness.

In situations where emotional harm is claimed, it might be necessary to present expert psychological testimony to convince the court of this fact. However, if the proponent of videotape presents such testimony, the opponent will probably demand the right to have an independent or adverse psychological examination of the child in order to convince the court that the child will not be traumatized by having to testify in court. The likely result is that the child will be traumatized by a process that was used to try to prevent trauma!

Fourth, many of these alternative techniques involving the use of videotape or closed-circuit television affect the defendant's right to confront the accuser. In child abuse cases, this usually involves the offender's right to a face-to-face cross-examination of the child in court. This is another hotly debated issue in our courts today. Some jurisdictions permit certain concessions; others do not. This issue should be avoided whenever possible.

The use of videotaped depositions, closed-circuit television, or some other alternative may spare the child the trauma of testifying in front of his or her abuser, but it could be harmful if the case is reversed on appeal and a new trial is ordered that requires live testimony months, if not years, later.

Fifth, if videotape or closed-circuit television is to be used, our advice is simple. Use it often, and do it well. Repetition and extensive experience bring competency and success. Use quality equipment. Develop a protocol that guides your use in ways that help develop expertise and a comfort level that increases the chances of obtaining reliable and credible information from the child.

Contact With the Defense: Negotiations

Cases that are well investigated and prepared for trial generally do not go to trial. They are resolved with a plea. To negotiate a case successfully, a prosecutor must be ready, willing, and able to try it. An experienced prosecutor who tries a lot of child abuse cases will get better dispositions than will prosecutors who have not had much experience or who are afraid to try these cases.

If the facts warrant that a concession be made to the offender, it is better to recommend dismissing a couple of counts from a multicount indictment rather than negotiating away the right to argue for the appropriate disposition. Naturally, there are some offenders who will not plead guilty or take responsibility for their behavior and who insist that the state prove them guilty beyond a reasonable doubt. Nevertheless, it is the prosecutor's responsibility to assess which cases can be resolved with a plea and which must be tried or dismissed. There are a number of factors that a prosecutor considers during this assessment.

First, what is the strength of the case? The answer to this question often depends on how good a witness the child will be. This is usually a prime consideration. If the child is likely to be a good witness and can withstand the rigors of testifying, the prosecutor is more likely to hold a firm line and demand pleas to the offenses charged, as well as the right to argue for whatever disposition the prosecutor believes appropriate.

However, if the child is not likely to make a good witness or would suffer significant harm by testifying, and if there is precious little corroborative evidence, then the prosecutor will likely offer concessions.

Concessions may take the form of dismissing some charges in exchange for a plea to others, amending to a less serious charge, or perhaps recommending a more lenient disposition than they would otherwise request. In rare cases, the concession will take the form of a dismissal.

Second, does the offender have a lengthy criminal history or a previous history of child sexual abuse or domestic violence? Are children in the community likely to be at risk (such as an offender holding a job that brings him or her in direct contact with children)? If the answers are yes, the prosecutor probably will not be inclined to reduce a charge or give up the opportunity to recommend a disposition at the time of sentencing.

A third factor to consider is, How much physical evidence exists to support the child's description of the abuse? Strong cases have corroborative evidence and are far less stressful for victims or witnesses in court because cross-examinations are not usually as harsh as in cases without corroborative evidence (he-said/she-said) cases.

Factual corroboration can be in the form of witnesses who independently verify aspects of a victim's disclosure, or perhaps confiscated diaries with detailed writings, work time cards, photographs, Vaseline™ jars, bank checks, or tape recordings.

Medical evidence corroboration can be such things as semen stains, bruising, or scar tissue that was found to be consistent with a crime victim's description.

Another aspect of the negotiation process involves consideration of the child's emotional state. It is extremely important to be honest and forthright with children when they ask, "What will happen to Dad (or Grandpa)?" It is not unusual for children to say that they don't want their abuser to go to jail. Sometimes, their requests can be accommodated. However, there are other cases in which the offender deserves lengthy incarceration regardless of the child's feelings.

It is important that we tell children the truth. Do not lie or mislead them when they ask what will happen to their abuser. The system should not perpetuate any form of maltreatment. Do your best to explain to the child that the decision as to whether Dad or Grandpa goes to jail is for the judge and the judge alone to make. Furthermore, it is not the child's fault if Dad goes to jail. It is Dad's fault! This is difficult, but it must be done.

Meeting With the Defense Lawyer or Investigator

It is not unusual for the defense attorney or his or her investigator to ask to speak with the child or other witnesses. This often occurs during the weeks immediately preceding the scheduled trial. With strong child witnesses, the prosecutor may actually want to arrange for such a meeting at the prosecutor's office, the child advocacy center, or some other neutral location. This meeting requires the personal attention of the case prosecutor and not the child advocate or child victim witness specialist, although they may be nearby or in attendance. Such a meeting may convince the defense attorney of the strength of the case and the child's abilities to be a competent and credible witness, and the defense attorney may very well be able to convince his or her client to enter a plea, thus avoiding a trial.

The prosecutor can offer to set up a meeting with defense counsel after consulting with the child, the child's counselor, and the child's parents. *However, the child should never be subjected to a face-to-face interview with the offender.*[1] It is important to acknowledge that both the defense attorney and the prosecutor have a legal and ethical obligation to encourage witnesses to be available to both sides. Likewise, it is important to note that witnesses, whether children or adults, do not have to talk with the opposing side if they do not want to.

Therefore, victims and their families should be told that if they are contacted by the defense, they should alert the prosecutor's office. The prosecutor's staff can act as a liaison between the defense and the child victim and his or her family with respect to any request for a meeting.

Trial Considerations and Testimonial Tips

Listed below are additional suggestions that might be helpful in dealing with child witnesses and may increase your chances of obtaining a favorable result at trial while minimizing the trauma to the child:

- Arrange to have as many breaks as possible during the child's testimony. These breaks should occur with the same regularity whether the child is on direct or cross-examination. Young children generally do not have an attention span that lasts longer than 20 to 30 minutes. Be assertive in court and ask for recesses, especially if you notice that the child is displaying signs of emotional distress or needing to take a break.
- When talking with child witnesses, keep your sentences short, direct, and to the point. It is better to ask several short questions rather than one long one.
- Use simple words such as "show me," "tell me about," and "said" instead of adult words such as "depict," "describe," and "indicated."
- Avoid the use of pronouns. Use the names and places that are familiar to the child. For example, do not ask, "Where did she go?" Instead, ask, "Where did Mary go?"
- Stay away from negatives and tag questions, such as, "You said this before, didn't you?" or "Isn't it true that . . .?"
- Avoid "yes/no" questions with multiple propositions, such as, "Do you remember coming to my office last August and sitting on my lap and telling me about what Uncle Dick did to you last summer?"
- Avoid asking children "Do you remember?" questions unless you are firmly convinced that the child understands what this means.

- Keep your thoughts concrete and literal. Children are very literal in their use of language and concepts. For example, the child's literal use of language may mean that the word "touch" describes only contact by a hand or a finger and not contact by other body parts. Similarly, the question "Did he touch you?" will not elicit a description of abuse if the child was the one doing the touching. Likewise, asking a child whether his or her "clothes" were on or off may not cover the situation in which his or her "pajamas" were removed. Finally, asking a child if anyone "hurt" him or her may not get at the abuse scenario, especially if the abuse was not painful.
- Be an active and aggressive advocate in the courtroom. The prosecutor can affect the mode of questioning so as to maximize efforts to obtain accurate and truthful testimony. Do not hesitate to object to overly aggressive, abusive, and confusing questioning by opposing counsel.
- Finally, be low-key and nonconfrontational in your exchange with opposing counsel or the trial judge in the presence of the child witness. Witnessing courtroom confrontation can be very upsetting to children and may make it difficult for them to concentrate on questions they are being asked in the midst of volatile exchanges.

Because the prosecutor is the one responsible for bringing the child abuse case to court, he or she must take a leadership role to ensure that the legal system is sensitive, responsive, and fair to child victims and witnesses, while also ensuring that the truth is obtained and justice is served.

Note

1. One possible exception involves cases where the offender represents him- or herself and your state mandates that the victim or witness be made available for an interview.

Appendix A:
A Case Status Letter—
First Notice

Date

Samuel and Rosalie Smith
2397 Sheridan Court
Kenosha, WI 53144

RE: State vs. John J. Zimmerfield
      DA File: 99 CF 1234
      Charges: Criminal Damage to Property, Theft, and Entry into a
                  Locked Vehicle

Dear Mr. and Mrs. Smith:

This letter is to inform you that the District Attorney's Office has begun a criminal prosecution in the above entitled case. As a witness in this case, you *may* be subpoenaed for a preliminary hearing and/or trial, however, most cases never go to trial. The testimony you may be able to provide will enable the judge and/or jury to determine what actually happened. As a witness, we respectfully request that you keep our office notified about any address or telephone number changes, please.

The District Attorney's Office has created the Victim/Witness Program to help victims and witnesses to understand the complex criminal justice system, and to find answers to as many questions as you may have about your role or involvement in this court case. Because your child may be a potential witness in this case (in the future), we will be assigning a victim/witness specialist to you and your child.

The victim/witness specialist assigned to your case will be in touch with you within the next day or two. He or she will want to answer any questions or address any concerns you or your family may have regarding the prosecution of this case. The victim/witness specialist will schedule appointments to meet with you, your child, and the case prosecutor. It is our goal to take very good care of you and your child.

We are sending some literature that explains what your crime victims' rights are, a synopsis of the criminal justice process, information about how parents can help when their child goes to court, and information about parking near the courthouse.

Please keep this letter with you. If you need information about this case before we talk again, give us the name of the defendant and our case file number (listed at the top of this letter). We will gladly try to answer your questions. It is our goal that you receive the best possible assistance during the weeks to come. Please feel free to call the victim/witness program staff at 414-653-2400 (Monday-Friday from 8:00 a.m.-5:00 p.m.) with any questions or concerns you may have before we contact you in the near future.

Case Information

Initial Appearance—was held this afternoon. A plea of not guilty was entered. Attorney Dexter Monitor is the case defense attorney. A preliminary hearing has been scheduled for August 18 at 9:15 a.m. Bond was set at $10,000.00 cash*. This means the defendant must post that total amount before he can be released.

> * A condition of a bond is that the defendant have no contact with Samuel Smith (DOB 2/12/62); Rosalie Smith (DOB 4/21/66); or D.S. (DOB 6/17/92) during the pendency of this court action. The court also ordered the defendant not consume any alcoholic beverages or non-prescribed drugs and not travel within 100 feet of the residence located at 2397 Sheridan Court.

Although we do not anticipate any problem with this defendant, we are enclosing copies of the bond order (and instructions to be followed) if any problems or bond violations need to be reported to law enforcement.

Thank you very much for your cooperation. We look forward to meeting with you in the near future.

Sincerely,

Lynn Copen, Director
Victim/Witness Program

Appendix B:
When Your Child Goes to Court:
How Parents Can Help

General Information for Parents

Going to court, and expecting to testify, is often stressful for *anyone*. Most people have very little contact with the criminal or juvenile justice system, and they get very nervous just thinking about going to court. This tension is often compounded when parents learn that their child will need to appear in court, and probably testify. It is very normal and natural for parents to be concerned about what their child will experience, and how they can help make this experience easier for their loved one.

After working with hundreds of parents and children in this situation, our office has seen and learned some things that people often find helpful, and we have listed some of them below:

1. *Figure out exactly who is nervous, and what they are nervous about.* Very often, we find that it is really the *parent* who is the nervous one. People are most nervous over the unknown. When you don't know what to expect (whom you will see, what will be done), it causes upsets. Children are very intuitive and will pick up on a parent's feelings. As a parent, you will need to know that your child will look to you for indications about how to feel about going to court.

Have you ever found yourself having to go to some event in a new city or location, and not knowing where you were going, who would be there, or what you'd be expected to do? Do you remember the uneasy feeling you had? Maybe you were unfamiliar with the highway exits, or route needed to find the correct building. Making one wrong turn and getting lost could cause you to become anxious and upset.

Going to court can sometimes be the same way. You may wonder, Where do I go? Where can I park my car? Who will be at this court hearing? What will happen? How long will it take? These are all very legitimate questions. Having information about what is going to happen can be calming—both for you, the parent/caregiver, as well as for your child. We will try to give you information to help you better understand what is going to happen.

After we talk, if you have questions about anything, please do feel free to call me or a member of the victim/witness program staff. We are here to help *you* or your child whenever you need us. Call the following number _____ and ask for _____.

Enclosed is a special workbook for your child titled *Getting Ready for Court: A Book for Children*. We want you to help your child read the workbook and talk with your child about what it says.

This child's court workbook was written for children ages 4-10. Children younger than age 4 can understand *some* of the information, and children over age 10 can also benefit from it (but will probably not like the large print). We used the large print so that very young children would not be intimidated with the words and letters.

Children can sometimes be nervous about something completely different from their parents. A parent may worry about the child being able to recall and talk about an experience, or about cross-examination by an eager defense lawyer. A child may be more concerned about knowing what to do if he or she needs to go to the bathroom while on the witness stand, or about making up missed school assignments, or about how *you* will handle listening to what he or she will say in court.

Many children tell us that they don't want to upset their parents, and worry about the parents having difficulty listening to what the children need to tell about what they saw, heard, or had happen to them. Children love their parents and worry about hurting them. This is one of the reasons that some children initially disclose being a victim or witness to someone other than the parent first. It can be very hard for a child to testify in court and watch his or her parents show pain or distress as they listen to their child's testimony.

Frequently, we find that many children are not nearly as worried about testifying in court as their parents are. Some children have reported, at a later time, that the experience was not so bad, or was even helpful.

    2. *Find ways to reassure your child that you are all just fine.* This does not mean saying you are not nervous, if you really are. But you need to let your child know that you want him or her to tell the truth and answer questions to the best of his or her ability, and no matter what, you are proud and love him or her. Talk to your child about being a bit nervous, too, and that you will go through this together.

Maybe you are not the person to hear the details of what the child saw, heard, or experienced (see above explanation about why), but encourage your child to talk about what is of concern to him or her with whomever he or she feels comfortable. We prefer that the child talk with the *lawyer* about the details or facts of a case, but talking about worries, fears, or concerns with you or trusted friends will help us all out a great deal.

We have found that children who talk about what is bothering them, and have a trusted person listening to them, seem to recover more easily and completely than children who do not talk about their thoughts and feelings. Let us know what your child needs, and we will do our best to help you all out.

It is common for parents to think it is better to just forget about what happened and not *let* a child discuss problems or feelings about what they saw, heard, or experienced when they bring up the issue. Our findings have been just the opposite. However, please refrain from forcing a child to talk about things or specific details about an event. Children *do need* to process the experience, and we strongly encourage children to speak with a skilled therapist or counselor. Many children process their experience quickly and need to meet with a professional counselor or therapist only a few times. Other children may need to see a counselor many times before they are able to take steps toward recovery.

Your child will be very "tuned in" to whatever mood or feeling *you* are showing. Try to appear calm and relaxed. Try to not telegraph your worries to your child. Be aware that children hear extremely well and may overhear you talking to someone else about your concerns. As a parent, I notice that my own child seems to listen best when I do not want him to overhear me talking. But, that is life with children.

3. *Listed below are a few tips to consider:*
   a. There may be some waiting involved while at the courthouse. As interesting as the courthouse may be at first, to be at this new and busy place very long can become quite boring. So, bring a friend with you to talk with just in case you wait.
   b. We have a bed with blankets and pillows for naps. Although it is very rare that any child will be at the courthouse long enough to need a nap, there may be other children in the family who need a rest while everyone is waiting. These napping supplies are in our special children's waiting area.
   c. There are vending machines (soda/coffee/juice as well as snacks) in the courthouse. You will also find several books, coloring items, movies/VCR for you and your child to use while waiting. Please feel free, however, to bring your own coloring books, favorite toy, snacks, or games your child may want to play with.

      If you are attending a preliminary hearing, even though these are heard quickly, you may find yourself waiting anywhere from 10 to 30 minutes before your case is called.

Jury trial waiting times will likely be longer. You may find yourself waiting half a day before your child testifies. Although we do our best to coordinate schedules so your child arrives at court a short time before he or she will need to testify, unforseen delays or problems sometimes happen that cause witnesses to have to wait longer than we would like. For this reason, we encourage you to bring in a favorite healthy snack for your child.

d.   Remind your child that he or she will be just fine. Be calm. All your child needs to remember when he or she goes into court is to tell the truth. When your child is done testifying, talk with him or her about his or her feelings, rather than what was said.

Try to not focus on winning . . . or a verdict or "guilty." What a judge or jury does is not in your control. You and your child *do* control going into court and doing the best job you possibly can.

e.   Give your child love and affection. Hugs are wonderful! Hugs work wonders before court, after court, and anytime in between. By the way, you may want to tell your child that *you* need a hug when you go to court, too.

f.   The night before you go to court, you and your child should try to relax as much as possible. Fix your favorite meal, or watch a movie that you all enjoy, or take nice warm bubble baths. Try to find ways to share some laughter. Everyone should try to get a good night's sleep. The morning of court, do your best to eat a good breakfast.

g.   The afternoon before court, you may want to stock up on healthy snacks (fruit, granola bars, juices). We have found that although people are rarely hungry before court, once it is over, they want to eat or nibble on food.

h.   Enclosed is a map that shows you where the courthouse is located and where there is free parking for witnesses.

Our office has professional victim/witness program staff available to you Monday through Friday. Someone from our team will be assigned as a "court friend" to help you and your child. Your court friend will cover all of this information with you in person, as well as try to answer any of your questions. We want parents to have all of this information in writing, because there is so much to know and remember!

If you ever have a question, concern, or need assistance, please feel free to call the person listed. If your assigned court friend is not available, just ask the receptionist to contact anyone in the victim/witness unit (we all help each other out whenever needed). We are here to help you and your child, and we want to make your court experience as easy and pleasant as possible. We may not have all of the answers to your questions right away, but we promise to try to get them as soon as possible. We are a team and need your help, too.

Thank you.

Appendix C:
Bond Conditions/
No Contact Orders

Information for Witnesses

Date:

State of _____ vs. (Defendant's name)

Court File Number: _____

Law Enforcement Agency Case Number: _____

Investigating Law Enforcement Agency & Telephone No: _____

Name of Prosecutor & Telephone No: _____

Name of Court Educator and Telephone No: _____

Court hearing dates (list if known): _____

Branch of Court/Assigned Judge: _____

Bond Information

A bond was set on (insert date) in the amount of (list amount). In addition to a (list bond amount), the defendant was ordered to have *no contact* with the following people and/or locations: (list names of people and/or addresses with which the defendant is ordered to have no contact while out of jail on a bond).

Violations of conditions of a bond are serious matters and should be reported to the above listed law enforcement agency immediately. Attached is a copy of the court bond order to show to law enforcement officers, in the event their assistance is necessary.

Additional bond conditions:

_____

_____

_____

Additional special instructions to witnesses:

_____

_____

_____

_____

_____

_____

_____

_____

_____

_____

Appendix D:
Child Victim Impact Statement

Dear Parent:

When a person is convicted of a crime, the judge will order what is called a *presentence investigative report* before the sentence is actually pronounced. The presentence investigative report is a long report written by someone from the Department of Corrections. Someone from the Department of Corrections will probably want to talk with you and your child about how this crime has affected your child's life.

Many people feel more comfortable writing a letter, and some children are more comfortable writing out a child's victim impact statement. Attached to this letter is a victim impact statement form for your child to complete, with your help. You can write a letter, complete this statement form, and talk with the presentence investigative agent. You can also choose to not write anything or talk with anyone about any of this. You have a right to choose to do what you wish.

A presentence investigative report is mostly about the defendant (the person convicted of committing a crime). But the judge wants to know what a victim has to say about how this crime affected him or her. The judge carefully reads what is written by child victims and their parents. Writing can be quite hard for some people, especially children. To make things a little easier, we have written down some questions that you and your child could think about answering. Please know that neither you nor your child needs to answer any questions. You also can write as much as you need to, and can use more paper if necessary.

Your letter and your child's responses to this victim impact statement will be given to the case lawyer (prosecutor), judge, defense lawyer, presentence agent, and the defendant.

There are some rules about letters that go to a judge. We will tell you about those rules as we list the questions for you to consider answering.

We would like children to express *their* thoughts on the child victim impact form. It is okay to have a grown-up help a child with the statement, but the thoughts and feelings should be those of the child. Parents are welcome to write their own victim impact statement or letter that contains their thoughts and feelings. We need the victim impact statements returned to our office within the next 10 days. So to help you, we have enclosed a self-addressed envelope for you to use.

Please give me a call if you wish to talk about this further, or have questions. My telephone number is _____.

CHILD VICTIM IMPACT STATEMENT
(with adult assistance)

State of Wisconsin   Court File Number:

      vs.

_____

Judge: _____

Prosecutor: _____

Defense Lawyer: _____

Sentencing Date: _____

Charge at the time of sentencing: _____

Potential penalty range at time of sentencing: _____

Name of person helping child complete this form: ____

Relationship of the helper to the child: _____

Name of victim: _____Age: _____

Before the judge tells the defendant what will happen to him or her, the judge will read the presentence investigative report and any letters or statements made by victims or parents of child victims. You can use as little or as much paper as you need. You can answer any, all, or none of the questions listed below. You do not have to say anything at all if you don't want to. It's okay. But if you *do* want to say something to the judge, now is the time to do that.

Questions to Answer

1. Were you hurt by this crime? Being "hurt" could mean having either your body hurt or your feelings hurt.

     Yes_____   No_____

   If you were hurt by this crime, the judge will want to know more about that from you. Some children are hurt physically, like a bruise, burn, or broken bone. Sometimes, children are hurt emotionally, like really hurt feelings or being really sad or mad. Some children are hurt both physically and emotionally. If you were hurt by this crime, please tell the judge about your hurt.

   _____

   _____

   _____

   _____

2. If you were hurt, did you have to see someone to help try to fix the hurt?

     Yes_____   No_____

   If you answered yes, please tell us who you went to and if you need to continue to see someone for help.

   _____

   _____

   _____

   _____

3. Are you worried or scared about anything to do with what happened to you?

     Yes_____   No_____

   Sometimes, children are worried or scared after they saw or heard something, or had something happen to them. If you are worried or scared about anything, the judge would like to know what worries or scares you. We don't know if the judge or anyone can help you with your worries or fears, but we will try. We need to know what your worries or fears are first. If you can, please tell us what you would like us to know.

4. What do you hope the judge will say the sentence will be?

   The judge will want to know what you think should happen to the defendant for this crime. Before you answer this question, you need to know the rules that the judge must follow for sentencing. Go back to the first page of this letter. We tell you what the judge is allowed to use as a sentence. That is where it says "potential penalty." The judge cannot sentence anyone to more than what the law says. We have told you what the most is that someone can get for a sentence. The judge can sentence someone to less than what is listed but not more. These are the rules that the judge needs to follow. If you don't understand what this means, ask a grown-up to help you, or call your court friend to help explain this to you.

The judge has to make the final decision about what a sentence will be, and may or may not do what you would like, but the judge will read your letter.

_____

_____

_____

_____

5. What are your feelings about everything that has happened in this case?
   We would like to know how you feel about all that has happened. Were you treated fairly by the police? Were you treated fairly by the District Attorney? Was your court friend helpful? What did you think about going to court? These are some of the things we would like to know about. You can tell us anything—good or bad—about going to court. We really want to know how you feel and how we can do a better job.

_____

_____

_____

_____

6. Is there anything else you want to say that was not asked? (Feel free to add more pages if you need to.)

_____

_____

_____

_____

7. Color any kind of picture you would like.

Appendix E:
Sample: Very Young Child
Victim Impact Statement

Dear Suzie:

It is your turn to tell the judge how you feel about what happened. You do not have to say anything if you don't want to.

Your mom said she would help you write a letter to the judge. Thank you for talking to us. Thank you for being a big help.

Questions

1. How did this crime make you feel? You can circle as many faces as you want. You can draw any face you want to.

    ☺ ☹ (add circles to show any other face you want to).

    What do you want the judge to say to (name of defendant)?

    _____

    _____

    _____

3. Is there anything else you want the judge to know about how you feel now?

    _____

    _____

    _____

4. Please draw us a picture of something you like:

Thank you for helping us. You were a big help.

Appendix F:
Court Educator Notes:
Work Product Checklist

Part 1—Parental Contact

Date:

Your name: _____

Defendant's name: _____

Child's name and age: _____

Case social worker/detective: _____

Parent/caregiver name: _____

Telephone number:_____Alternate phone: _____

Address: _____

Child's school: _____

Added information: _____

Discuss with parents and list their comments:

- Explain who you are

- Explain your role

- Discuss case status (precharging stage, charges, likely hearing dates)

- Identify any safety or security concerns:

    No concerns_____ Yes_____ If yes, identify and specify concerns:

    _____

    _____

    _____

    _____

Will law enforcement action be needed at this time (security intervention)?
No_____ Yes_____

If yes, what agency is being contacted, and what action is requested or expected?

_____

_____

_____

_____

Are there parental concerns?   No_____   Yes_____   If yes, indicate the concerns:

_____

_____

_____

_____

Does the parent identify any disabilities, impairments, or other special difficulties or issues for this child?   No_____   Yes_____   If yes, explain:

_____

_____

_____

_____

Has the child expressed worries or fears to the parent about the case or going to court?   No_____   Yes_____   If yes, explain:

_____

_____

_____

_____

Will this child witness likely need extra time for assessment or preparation work?   No_____   Yes_____   If yes, what are the reasons for the more than average time? How much extra time is suggested?

_____

_____

_____

_____

Explain the overall purpose for the educational preparation sessions with the child and parent. Address the following:

1. How the introduction will initially take place between the "court friend" and the parent and child.
2. Discuss the gradual separation of the parent and child.
3. Discuss the parent meeting with the case lawyer, if separation happens safely.
4. Advise the parent to keep a list of questions and to bring the questions to the education and preparation appointment.

Document the literature that was given to the parent and/or child (check):

_____ Criminal justice system overview

_____ Victims' rights packet information

_____ *Getting Ready for Court*—workbook

_____ *Finding Your Way*—adolescent book

_____ Trauma information

_____ Letter to parents about children going to court

_____ Crime victim compensation

_____ Community resources for therapy and/or education

_____ Other (list):

What is the child's best time of day? _____

What is the child's worst time of day? _____

Child's support network (Who will be the primary support people for this child during the court process?): _____

_____

Scheduled appointment date and time for child and parent

Date and time: _____

Additional appointment date and time for child and parent:

_____

_____

_____

Other comments: _____

_____

_____

_____

Part 2—Child Contact Checklist

- Rapport Building

  What does this child like and/or dislike?

  _____

  _____

  _____

  _____

- Explain work time and no-work time rules to the child (show the timer).
- Child's ability to separate from a parent/caregiver (check):

  _____ Did so easily

  _____ Did so with some difficulty

  _____ Unable to separate or very difficult

  _____ Pretrial motions may be necessary to address the issue of a supporter
  or parent needed in court when the child testifies. Comments:

  _____

  _____

  _____

  _____

- Review the workbook with the child:

  _____ Identify the job function and role of: judge, jury, prosecutor, defense
  lawyer, bailiff, court reporter, court clerk, guardian ad litem

  _____ Child appears to understand the names and roles of the above-listed
  court people

  _____ Child has limited understanding about the roles of the above-listed court
  people

  _____ Child is unable to understand the roles of the above-listed court people

  _____ List any difficulties encountered with the workbook:

  _____

  _____

  _____

- Let the child wear a replica judge robe.
- Show the child the model miniature courtroom and have the child make his or
  her court doll, as well as any representation doll he or she wishes.

Discuss the following tasks and concepts with the child:

Telling the truth

Talking clearly and loudly

Using a microphone

Using the words "yes" and "no," rather than a shake/nod or "uh-huh," "uh-uh"

Court reporter needing to hear words clearly

Permission to correct any mistakes made, at any time, by either adults or the child

Guessing at answers

Repeated questions

Permission to say certain words in court

How to ask for a break when needed

Where the toilets are located

How to do deep, slow breathing

Holding or rubbing rocks, pennies, or representational dolls when nervous

Discuss the hard questions:
1. Time questions
   _____ Child can tell the time by the clock
   _____ Child not able to tell time by the clock
   _____ Child understands seconds, minutes, hours, days, weeks
   _____ Child does not understand time concepts (explain)

Will the child have difficulty with "how long something lasted" questions?

No_____ Yes_____ Explain: _____

_____

_____

_____

Will the child have difficulty with "how much time" questions?

No_____ Yes_____ If yes, explain: _____

_____

_____

_____

2. Distance questions (Can the child understand these words?):

_____ Near

_____ Far

_____ Close

3. Measurement questions (Does the child understand these forms of measurement or difference between a foot as something having toes and a foot as 12 inches? Does the child understand the difference between a yard being 36 inches or something you play in at your house?):

_____ Inch

_____ Foot

_____ Yard

_____ Height

_____ Weight

Will the child be able to answer "how far away or how close" questions?

No_____ Yes_____

Comments: _____

_____

_____

4. Comparison questions (Does the child understand what they mean?):

_____ Taller vs. smaller

_____ Bigger vs. smaller or "littler"

_____ More than vs. less than

_____ Older vs. younger

Comments: _____

_____

_____

5. Number questions

Does the child count by rote or script?   No_____ Yes_____

Does the child understand what the number represents?   No_____ Yes_____

Will the child be able to answer "how many times?" questions accurately?

No_____ Yes_____

Comments: _____

_____

_____

6. Relationship questions

Does this child understand the concept of close/far/near?   No____ Yes____

Does this child understand people relationships, such as aunt, uncle, cousin, brother, sister, mother, father, stepmother, stepfather?   No____   Yes____

Comments:

_____

_____

_____

Discuss the following common words or word combinations asked of witnesses in court. Does this witness demonstrate the ability to understand what is meant by these words when used in common sentences? These are common and sometimes confusing word/word combinations used by lawyers in court. List comments beside each word as needed for future reference:

____ Over

____ Under

____ Beside

____ Next to

____ On top of

____ Right

____ Wrong

____ "Do you remember . . .?" questions

____ Truth

____ Lie

____ Fib

____ Good

____ Bad

____ Trouble

____ Pretend

____ "If I were to (say or do . . .)"

____ Yesterday, today, tomorrow

Comments:

_____

_____

_____

Tour an actual courtroom

Does the child state any concerns, worries, fears, or comments about the courtroom, courtroom people, or courtroom environment? No____ Yes____

If yes, explain: _____

_____

_____

_____

How long can the child work without needing a break (attention span)?

Will there be any concern about the need for pretrial motions to alter the courtroom environment? No____ Yes____

If yes, explain: _____

_____

_____

_____

Is there anything the child wishes to talk about that was not discussed?

No____ Yes____

Comment/final comments:

_____

_____

_____

_____

_____

_____

_____

_____

_____

_____

_____

_____

_____

_____

_____

_____

_____

Appendix G:
Notice of Motion and
Notice of Motion to Limit the
Examination of Child Witness

State of Wisconsin	Circuit Court	Kenosha County

State of Wisconsin	:	
Plaintiff,	:	
v.	:	Case No: _____ CF_____
JOSEPH P.	:	
Defendant	:	

NOTICE OF MOTION AND MOTION TO LIMIT THE EXAMINATION OF CHILD WITNESS C.M.P. TO AGE APPROPRIATE LANGUAGE, GRAMMAR AND SENTENCE STRUCTURE

PLEASE TAKE NOTICE that on the 17th date of October, 19__, at 2:30 p.m., before the Honorable Michael S. Fisher, Circuit Court Branch 4, the plaintiff, State of Wisconsin, through its attorneys, Assistant District Attorneys Thomas J. Fallon and Shelly J. Rusch, will move the court pursuant to § 901.04 and 906.11 of the Wisconsin Statutes for an order:

Limiting the direct and cross examination of child witness C.M.P., whose date of birth is __/__/__, to age appropriate language, grammar, and sentence structure.

AS GROUNDS THEREFORE, and in support of this motion, the State relies on § 906.11, Stats. and the supporting memorandum with attachment.

Dated at Kenosha, Wisconsin, this 15th day of October 19____.

Respectfully submitted,

_____   _____
SHELLY J. RUSCH   THOMAS J. FALLON
Assistant District Attorney   Deputy District Attorney

Kenosha County Courthouse
912 56th Street
Kenosha, WI 53140-3747

Appendix H:
Memorandum in Support
of Motion in Limine

STATE OF WISCONSIN   CIRCUIT COURT   KENOSHA COUNTY

STATE OF WISCONSIN,   Case Number _____ CF_____

Plaintiff

v.

JOSEPH P.,

Defendant

It is within the discretionary power of the trial court to limit the language, grammar, and sentence structure used in the examination of child witnesses so that their examination will be effective for the ascertainment of the truth.

Section 906.11 of the Wisconsin Statutes reads as follows:

906.11 **Mode and order of interrogation and presentation (1)** CONTROL BY JUDGE. The judge shall exercise reasonable control over the mode and order of interrogating witnesses and presenting evidence so as to:

a) make the interrogation and presentation effective for the ascertainment of the truth,

b) avoid needless consumption of time, and

c) protect witnesses from harassment or undue embarrassment.

If the court limits the language, grammar, and sentence structure used in the examination of C.M.P. to age-appropriate concepts, the court will a) increase the likelihood of obtaining accurate information; b) save time by shortening and simplifying her testimony; and c) protect C.M.P. from harassment or undue embarrassment resulting from her inability to understand and respond accurately to adult language, mannerisms, and syntax. The arguments in support of this request are as follows:

First, C.M.P. has been in speech therapy classes while attending school in the Kenosha Unified School District. Recently, she was examined by Speech Therapist Gerald _____. A copy of his report is attached. Mr. _____ details some of C.M.P.'s linguistic abilities and impairments in this report. As a result, the State requests that any questioning of C.M.P.:

    a)   Be done in a soft non-intimidating voice since loud, harsh, and/or sarcastic commentary will hinder communicative efforts; and

    b)   Be stated in short sentences using simple verbs such as "tell me about," or "show me," since they are more effective than longer sentences using complex verbs which would be confusing to C.M.P.; and

    c)   Be done at a slow rate of speech and allow sufficient time for C.M.P. to answer the questions before attempting to ask additional questions; i.e., preclude "rapid fire" questions which could be confusing and misinterpreted.

Second, C.M.P. is a child who has suffered significant psychological harm at the hands of this defendant, her biological father, and her stepfather, Donald H., who is also charged with similar crimes as set forth in Kenosha County Circuit Court file No. __CF__. C.M.P. was approximately three years of age at the onset of abuse. C.M.P.'s older sister, C.E.P., was ten years of age. C.M.P. presented with positive medical findings for physical, as well as sexual abuse. C.M.P. is speech impaired, developmentally delayed, and although almost seven years of age, often functions at the level of a three-and-one-half to a four-and-one-half year old. She also has attention deficit disorder. As a result of these disabilities, there are many words, phrases, and concepts that C.M.P. is not capable of understanding. Also, the examination of C.M.P. in a hostile, loud manner will be ineffective in obtaining accurate information. The State is prepared to present expert psychological testimony if necessary to demonstrate the extent of the emotional trauma sustained by C.M.P.

Third, and by analogy, § 967.04(a)(1-10), Stats., which governs the use of video deposition testimony of children in lieu of live testimony is supportive. In considering whether a court should permit a video deposition of a child the court must take into account the linguistic and cognitive capabilities, as well as the emotional needs of a child. When scheduling a deposition, the court should take into consideration the child's maximum energy level and attention span; the place where the deposition is to take place; i.e., private, informal, and comfortable; determine the child's verbal skills and developmental level in connection with qualifying the child to testify; explain to the child the purpose of the hearing and explain the identity of the people present in order to place the child at ease; permit any party questioning the child to procure the assistance of an advisor who may, with the court's permission, conduct questioning; and finally, permit the child to testify from a position in the courtroom where the child is comfortable and supervise the spatial arrangements of the room and the location and movement of all people in attendance. These same factors should be taken into consideration when a child is expected to provide live testimony in front of a jury and a courtroom full of spectators.

Fourth, the American Bar Association's *Guidelines for the Fair Treatment of Child Witnesses in Cases where Child Abuse is Alleged (July 1985)* provides in part:

3. In criminal cases and juvenile delinquency and child protection proceedings where child abuse is alleged, court procedures and protocol should be modified as necessary to accommodate the needs of child witnesses including:

   - leading questions may be utilized under direct examination of child witnesses subject to the court's direction and control;
   - to avoid intimidation or confusion of a child witness, examination and cross-examination should be carefully monitored by the presiding judge;
   - when necessary, the child should be permitted to testify from a location other than that normally reserved for witnesses who testify in the particular courtroom;
   - a person supportive of the child witness should be permitted to be present and accessible to the child at all times during his or her testimony, but without influencing the child's testimony.

Fifth, it is now axiomatic that a criminal defendant must have the services of an interpreter if the defendant does not understand or speak English well enough to confer with his lawyer or understand the testimony. *State v. Neave,* 117 Wis. 2d 359, 344 N.W. 2d 181 (1984).

Fairness requires that criminal defendants have the assistance of interpreters to avoid questions of effective assistance of counsel, whether inability to understand testimony resulted in a loss of the right to effective cross-examination, and to avoid the feeling of having been dealt with unfairly which may arise when language barrier renders all or part of the trial incomprehensive. *Neave,* at 365. It is time, and in the interests of justice to treat child victims and witnesses with equal respect. It is fundamentally unfair to expect a child to communicate in court on an adult level. Children are developmentally incapable of effectively communicating on an adult level—especially in court; just like the defendant who does not speak or comprehend English. We provide the means for defendants to effectively communicate in court and we should do the same for the child victims and witnesses.

Finally, there are sound policy reasons which not only permit, but actually instruct a court to limit the method and mode of interrogating child witnesses to age appropriate concepts. For example, the Wisconsin Supreme Court has opined:

The circuit court should, however, use the tools available to the criminal justice system to eliminate or lessen the burden on B.P. while making her testimony available in the criminal proceeding. . . . B.P. is a child who has suffered greatly. The legal system should not add to her suffering. . .

A circuit court has power, within constitutional limits, to alter courtroom procedures to protect the emotional well-being of the child witness.

State v. Gilbert, 109 Wis 2d 5011, 516-17, 326 N.W. 2d 744 (1982). *See also* 3 Wigmore Evidence, § 781, at 173 (Chadborn ed. 1970) where

(a)n intimidating <u>manner</u> in putting questions may so coerce or disconcern the witness that his answers do not represent his actual knowledge on the subject. . . . So also questions which . . . <u>cause embarrassment, shame, or anger</u> may unfairly lead him to such demeanor and utterance that the impression produced by his statements does not do justice to his real testimonial value.

(Emphasis in original).

Dated this ____day of October 19___.
Respectfully submitted,

_____
Thomas J. Fallon
Deputy District Attorney

_____
Shelly J. Rusch
Assistant District Attorney

Kenosha County Courthouse
912 - 56th Street
Kenosha, WI 53140-3747
262-653-2400

Attorneys for Plaintiff

Appendix I:
Speech Therapy Observations

NAME:

DATE:

BIRTH DATE:

CHRONOLOGICAL AGE: years

_____ has been enrolled in speech therapy since May, 1988; she had been enrolled in the Early Childhood Program from May __ 1988 to June __ 1990. _____ is
presently receiving speech therapy in a small group setting three days a week at

_____ School. She is in the first grade where her teacher reports she is having difficulty in all academic areas. _____ is receiving special instruction in a small group
setting with the reading specialist.

_____ over-all language skills are delayed from six months to possibly three years in
the area of expressive vocabulary. Her language skills are difficult to assess because
of variances in behavior which may affect standardized test scores. When con-
fronted with a situation in which she feels she is not succeeding, _____ reverts to
immature behaviors which might include unselective pointing, inattention, and increased random movements.

_____ is a verbal child who enjoys talking, especially if she can control the topic.
Self-initiated communication appears at a higher level than when asked direct
questions. Informal testing, as well as teacher and speech therapist observations,
suggest _____ functional language skills appear to be that of a child between four
and five years of age. The more comfortable _____ is in a speaking situation, the
more apt she is to express herself appropriately.

In eliciting information, the following guidelines will be helpful in helping _____
express herself more accurately:

1. The importance of non-verbal communication should not be overlooked. If an intimidating voice (loud, harsh, sarcastic, etc.) is used to question _____, she may respond to that rather than the actual question. Facial expressions and other body language may be considered intimidating and cause _____ to respond inappropriately and/or immaturely.

2. Questions should be stated in short sentences when possible. "Tell me about . . ." "Show me . . ." and "Tell me more" are more effective than long questions which may tend to be confusing ("What happened three months ago when you were at home?")

3. When questioning _____, speak at a slow rate of speech. Questions which are rapidly fired at her could be confusing and misinterpreted. Also, _____ should be given time to respond to the question. A brief latency period will provide _____ with time to process the question. Because of distractibility and inattentiveness, it may be necessary to repeat a question more than once. When possible, the same question should be restated in different words.

4. The use of concrete vocabulary is critical to comprehension of any statement or question. Temporal (time) concepts are difficult for _____. She understands the days of the week and the concepts of yesterday and tomorrow. However, questions related to last month or last year are more abstract and could be confusing to _____. The concept of "remember" is also difficult for _____. A simple statement "Tell me about . . ." is more effective than "Try to remember what happened."

On October 16, 19__, _____ was administered the *Boehm Test of Basic Concepts*. This test examines a child's ability to comprehend fifty basic concepts a child should know when entering first grade. _____ comprehended 41 of the 50 concepts. Those missed included: beginning, below, medium-sized, forward, pair, skip, equal, in order, and least. The 41 concepts _____ did understand in the test situation included:

top	over	row	not first/last
through	widest	different	never
away from	most	after	matches
next to	between	almost	always
inside	whole	half	right
some, not many	nearest	center	zero
middle	second	as many	above
few	corner	side	every
farthest	several	other	separated
around	behind	alike	left
			third

It would appear that _____ can communicate her experiences if concrete questions are asked using vocabulary which can be understood by a child of four to five years of age. Questioning should be presented in a non-threatening manner accompanied with a slow rate of speech.

A major concern of this speech therapist is that _____ may become unable to linguistically process questions as she becomes emotionally involved with the questions. She may elect not to express herself, become unable to answer, or begin engaging in immature behaviors, such as rocking in her chair, making "silly" comments, or covering her face with her hands in an attempt to avoid answering questions. I am sure these behaviors will be taken into consideration as _____ attempts to express herself verbally.

_____

Speech Therapist

Appendix J:
Motion in Limine Attachment

Child Witnesses in Abuse Cases
JULY 1985

BE IT RESOLVED, that the American Bar Association approves the "Guidelines for the Fair Treatment of Child Witnesses in Cases Where Child Abuse is Alleged":

A TEAM APPROACH

1. A multidisciplinary team involving the prosecutor, police and social services resource personnel should be utilized in the investigation and prosecution of cases where a child is alleged to be a victim or witness to abuse in order to reduce the number of times that a child is called upon to recite the events involved in the case as well as to create a feeling of trust and confidence in the child.

   Members of such teams should receive specialized training in the investigation and prosecution of cases where children are alleged victims and witnesses of abuse.

   Whenever possible, the same prosecutor should be assigned to handle all aspects of a case involving an alleged child victim or witness including related proceedings outside the criminal justice system.

A SPEEDY TRIAL

2. In all proceedings involving an alleged child victim, the court should take appropriate action to ensure a speedy trial in order to minimize the length of time a child must endure the stress of his or her involvement in the proceeding. In ruling on any motion or request for a delay or continuance of a proceeding involving an alleged child victim, the court should consider and give weight to any potential adverse impact the delay or continuance may have on the well being of a child.

PROCEDURAL REFORM

3. In criminal cases and juvenile delinquency and child protection proceedings where child abuse is alleged, court procedures and protocol should be modified as necessary to accommodate the needs of child witnesses including:

> If the competency of the child witness is in question, the court evaluate competency on an individual basis without resort to mandatory or arbitrary age limits.

> Leading questions may be utilized on direct and cross-examination of a child witness subject to the court's direction and control.

> To avoid intimidation or confusion of a child witness, examination and cross-examination should be carefully monitored by the presiding judge.

> When necessary, the child should be permitted to testify from a location other than that normally reserved for witnesses who testify in the particular courtroom.

> A person supportive of the child witness should be permitted to be present and accessible to the child at all times during his or her testimony, but without influencing the child's testimony.

> The child should be permitted to use anatomically detailed dolls and drawings during his or her testimony.

> When necessary, the child should be permitted to testify via closed-circuit television or through a one-way mirror so long as the defendant's right to cross-examine is not impaired.

> Persons not necessary to the proceedings should be excluded from the courtroom at the request of the child witness or his or her representative during pretrial hearings in cases where the child is alleged to be the victim of physical, emotional or sexual abuse.

> At pretrial hearings and in child protection proceedings the court, in its discretion, if necessary to avoid the repeated appearance of a child witness, may allow the use of reliable hearsay.

> When necessary the court should permit the child's testimony at a pretrial or noncriminal hearing to be given by means of a videotaped deposition.

LEGISLATIVE INITIATIVE

4. State legislature should, where necessary, enact appropriate legislation to permit modification of court procedures and evidentiary rules as suggested herein and in addition should:

> extend the statute of limitations in cases involving the abuse of children;

> establish programs to provide special assistance to child victims and witnesses or enhance existing programs to improve the handling of child abuse cases and minimize the trauma suffered by child victims, in cooperation with local communities and the federal government.

MEDIA RESPONSIBILITY

5. The public has a right to know and the news media have a right to report about crimes where children are victims and witnesses; however, the media should use restraint and prudent judgment in reporting such cases and should not reveal the identity of a child victim.

Special Legal Issues: Selected References

George v. Commonwealth, 885 S.W. 2d 938 (Ky. 1994)—Closed circuit television: elements

> The court held that the trial court committed reversible error when it allowed the appellant's daughter, a nonvictim witness, to testify via closed-circuit television. The statute applies only to victims, not witnesses.

Guaranty Development Co. v. Liberstein, 83 A.2d 669 (DC 1951)— Judge's control of courtroom environment

> "It is well settled that the mode of conducting trials and the order of introducing evidence are matters belonging very largely to the practice of the court, and a departure from the usual will not be a ground for reversal unless it appears it worked serious injury to the opposite party."

Hemphill v. State, 826 S.W. 2d 730 (Tex. Ct. App. 1992)—Anatomical dolls; videotaped depositions or testimony

> Court properly admitted the videotaped testimony of the complaining witness, who was 4 years old at the time of the videotaping. Because the state called the witness during its case-in-chief and the defendant cross-examined him, there was no violation of the defendant's confrontation rights.

The author wishes to specifically thank senior attorneys Brian K. Holmgren and Victor Veith, from the American Prosecutors Research Institute, National Center for the Prosecution of Child Abuse (the nonprofit research and technical assistance affiliate of the National District Attorney's Association), for their enormous assistance in both critiquing and editing this book and by providing the legal case information and citations for lawyers and court educators contained herein.

Hicks-Bey v. United States, 649 A.2d 569 (DC 1994)—Closed-circuit television: constitutionality

This case concerned the judge's ability to control the conduct of the proceedings . . . to ensure that the proper decorum and appropriate atmosphere are established, that all parties are treated fairly, and that justice is done. Indeed, innovative trial procedures are acceptable as long as they are "administered carefully and meet the requirements of due process."

Hopkins v. State, 632 So. 2d 1372 (Fla. 1994)—Failure of trial court to make individualized specific findings; closed-circuit television: constitutionality

The trial court failed to make specific findings of fact that the child victim would suffer emotional or mental harm if required to testify in the presence of the defendant before allowing closed-circuit television testimony. The trial court merely adopted the testimony of the child's mother and the psychologist, who both claimed that the child would be emotionally harmed if forced to testify in open court, and the court made no individualized determination of necessity.

Nunn v. State, 845 P.2d 435 (Alaska Ct. App. 1994)—Videotaped depositions or testimony

Defendant's conviction of second-degree sexual abuse of a minor was supported by properly admitted videotape of victim's interview with police detective, to show victim's demeanor when making statements inconsistent with trial testimony in which she recanted allegations of abuse by defendant.

People v. Guce, 560 N.Y.S. 2d 53 (NY. App. Div. 1990)—Closed-circuit television: threats and trauma

To determine whether the use of closed-circuit television testimony was proper, the court examined several factors: The crime was committed in a particularly heinous manner; the child witnesses were particularly young (ages 6 and 8); the defendant, their father, occupied a position of authority with respect to the witnesses; there was an express threat by their mother that they would be responsible for the incarceration of their father and the dissolution of their family f they continued to cooperate with the prosecution; and the children felt abandoned by both their father and mother and would be particularly susceptible to psychological harm if required to testify in open court or in the physical presence of the defendant. Therefore, the record amply supported the use of live, two-way, closed-circuit television in this case.

State v. Andrews, 447 N.W. 2d 118 (Iowa 1989)—Competence: generally; videotaped depositions or testimony

That trial court had previously determined that the 4-year-old child sexual abuse victim was competent to testify did not prevent the court from later determining that the victim was incompetent to testify at the retrial of the defendant. At the new trial, the judge found that the victim lacked the competency to be a witness because she demonstrated an inability to formulate intelligent answers or communicate impressions and recollections regarding the abuse; she was unresponsive to simple, straightforward questions; and she did not verbalize any independent recollection or details surrounding the alleged incidents. The court found that the trial court had properly recognized and accommodated the developmental limitations associated with a child of her age.

State v. Barber, 494 N.W. 2d 497 (Minn. Ct. App. (1993)—Videotaped depositions or testimony

Evidence—including testimony of the 7-year-old alleged victim, videotaped interview, and victim's statements to mother consistently indicating defendant had inserted his finger into her vagina—was sufficient to support conviction of first-degree sexual conduct.

State v. Crandall, 577 A.2d 483 (N.J. 1990)—Closed-circuit television: trauma

The trial court found that there was substantial likelihood of severe emotional upset and psychological upset and ruled that a psychiatric evaluation was not necessary for the court to reach that conclusion. The New Jersey Supreme Court held that the trial court's findings that the victim would be traumatized by testifying in the presence of the defendant were sufficient to justify the use of closed-circuit television. Expert testimony was not required to justify the use of closed-circuit television.

State v. Johnson, 528 N.E.2d 567 (Ohio App. 1986)—Judge's control of courtroom environment

The trial judge did not only what he was authorized, but required, to do. He made a decision to exercise reasonable control over the mode of interrogating the infant-witness with a view to making the interrogation and presentation effective for the ascertainment of truth while protecting the witness from undue embarrassment.

State v. Kirchbaum, No. 94-0899-CR, 1995 Wisc. App. LEXIS 672 (Wis. Ct. App. May 25, 1995)—Videotaped depositions or testimony

The court properly admitted a videotaped deposition of a child witness that was taken prior to a previous trial on the same charge at the subsequent trial.

State v. Lomprey, 496 N.W. 2d 172 (Wis. Ct. App. 1992)—Anatomical dolls; videotape depositions or testimony

The court found that the admission of videotaped deposition—in which the alleged child sexual abuse victim manifested her fear of the defendant by withdrawing into a shell immediately upon the defendant's entrance into the room—did not violate the defendant's confrontation rights, and testimonial conduct was not hearsay but, rather, the functional equivalent of live, in-court testimony. The 3-year-old child's out-of-court testimonial acts, in undressing anatomically correct dolls and using them to illustrate the defendant's alleged sexual abuse, possessed sufficient indicia of reliability to satisfy confrontation clause requirements, where the child had never seen anybody having sexual contact and had no basis for knowing about such conduct, and a witness who recounted the child's actions testified that the child undressed the dolls spontaneously without any prompting from the witness.

State v. Menzies, 603 A.2d 419 (Conn. 1992)—Judge's control of court environment

The court did not abuse discretion in permitting the guardian ad litem to sit with an 8-year-old victim during testimony where testimony from three witnesses supported the position that the presence of the GAL would facilitate in-court testimony.

The court also rejected the defendant's claim that the presence of the GAL enhanced the victim's credibility and heightened sympathy for her, noting that the trial court appropriately gave a curative instruction to the jury members that they were not to draw any inferences from this, and that the presence of a support person was to facilitate the testimony by placing the child at ease in the court setting.

In addition, the court upheld restrictions on people permitted to be in court during the child's testimony, the use of leading questions on direct, and restrictions on cross-examination pursuant to State's statutory provisions.

State v. Rogers, 692 P.2d 2 (Mont. 1984)—Support person with child witness

Pursuant to Rule 611, the trial court was well within its discretion in allowing the 4-year-old victim to sit on the prosecuting attorney's lap. That posture assisted in directing the victim's attention to the questioning and provided comfort to her during a difficult and unfamiliar experience.

State v. Twist, 528 A.2d 1250 (Me. 1987)—Unavailability; face-to-face confrontation: videotaped depositions or testimony

The court held that considerations of public policy and necessity warranted dispensing with direct, face-to-face confrontation between the defendant and the children at the time of the videotaping of their testimony. The defendant was concealed behind a one-way mirror, maintained constant communication with his attorney through audio hook-up, and was allowed to view the videotape simultaneously on a monitor. The court determined that the children were unavailable because they would suffer severe emotional trauma if required to testify; their testimony was sufficiently trustworthy because the children understood the serious nature of their testimony and the requirement to tell the truth; and there was corroborating evidence.

United States v. Lyons, 33 M.J. 543 (A.C.M.R. 1992)—Disabled victim: competency; videotaped deposition or testimony

A deaf, mute, mentally retarded victim was found competent to testify. The victim's sign language vocabulary did not exceed 200 words, which she augmented by pointing, gesturing, and grunting. The court also admitted a videotape in which the victim reenacted the incident. The introduction of the videotape did not deny the defendant's right of confrontation because the victim was subject to cross-examination at trial. The defendant's cross-examination of the victim was effective because the victim was competent to testify.

United States v. Thompson, 31 M.J. 168 (CMA 1990)—Face-to-face confrontation

The court has inherent authority to dispense with face-to-face confrontation upon proper showing of necessity. Two boys sodomized by their father were permitted to testify from a chair in the middle of the courtroom with their backs to the defendant.

References and Suggested Reading

Berliner, L., & Conte, J. R. (1995). The effects of disclosure and intervention on sexually abused children. *Child Abuse & Neglect, 19*(3), 371-384.

Chambers, K. (1995). Social policy implications. In A. Tobey, G. Goodman, J. Batterman-Faunce, H. Orcutt, & T. Sachsenmaier (Eds.), *Balancing the rights of children and defendants: Accuracy and jurors' perceptions in memory and testimony in the child witness.* Thousand Oaks, CA: Sage.

Conte, J. (1986). *A look at child sexual abuse* [Booklet]. South Deerfield, MA: National Committee to Prevent Child Abuse.

Copen, L., & Pucci, L. (1999). *Getting ready for court: A workbook for children.* Thousand Oaks, CA: Sage.

Dziech, B. W., & Schudson, C. B. (1989). *On trial: America's courts and their treatment of children.* Boston: Beacon Press.

Goodman, G. S., & Bottoms, B. (1993). *Child victims, child witnesses: Understanding and improving testimony.* New York: Guilford.

Goodman, G. S., Taub, E. P., Jones, D. P. H., England, T., Port, L. K., Rudy, L., & Prado, L. (1992). Testifying in criminal court: Emotional effects on child sexual assault victims. *Monograph of the Society for Research in Child Development, 57*(5).

Johnson Institute. (1993). *Tulip doesn't feel safe—Helping kids deal with unsafe situations* [Videotape]. Minneapolis, MN: Author.

Lamb, S., & Edgar-Smith, S. (1994). *Journal of Interpersonal Violence, 9,* 307-326.

Lawson, L., & Chaffin, M. (1992). False negatives in sexual abuse disclosure interviews: Incidence and influence of caretaker's belief in abuse in cases of accidental abuse discovery by diagnosis of STD. *Journal of Interpersonal Violence, 7,* 532-542.

Lipovsky, J. A. (1994). The impact of court on children: Research findings and practical recommendations. *Journal of Interpersonal Violence, 9,* 238-257.

Lipovsky, J. A., & Stern, P. (1997). Preparing children for court: An interdisciplinary view. *Child Maltreatment, 2,* 150-163.

Lyon, T. D. (1996). Assessing children's competence to take the oath: Research and recommendations. *APSAC Advisor, 9*(1), 1-6.

MacFarlane, K. (1986). *Helping parents cope with extrafamilial molestation in sexual abuse of young children.* New York: Guilford.

Maroules, N., & Reynard, C. (1993). *Voir dire in child-victim sex trials: A strategic guide for prosecutors.* Springfield: Illinois State's Attorney Appellate Prosecutor Child Witness Project.

McGough, L. (1994). *Child witnesses: Fragile voices in the American legal system.* New Haven, CT: Yale University Press.

Morison, S., & Greene, E. (1992). Juror and expert knowledge of child sexual abuse. *Child Abuse & Neglect, 16,* 595-613.

Myers, J. E. B. (1992). *Evidence in child abuse and neglect* (2nd ed.). New York: Wiley.

Myers, J. E. B., Goodman, G. S., & Saywitz, K. J. (1996). Psychological research on children as witnesses: Practical implications for forensic interviews and courtroom testimony. *Pacific Law Journal, 28*(1), 3-91.

National Center for Prosecution of Child Abuse. (1993). *Investigation and prosecution of child abuse* (2nd ed.). Alexandria, VA: National District Attorneys Association, American Prosecutors Research Institute.

On prosecutorial ethics. (1986). *Hastings Constitutional Law Quarterly, 13,* 538-539.

Perry, N. W., & Wrightsman, L. S. (1991). *The child witness: Legal issues and dilemmas.* Newbury Park, CA: Sage.

Pucci, L., & Copen, L. (2000). *Finding your way: What happens when you tell about abuse.* Thousand Oaks, CA: Sage.

Sas, L., Hurley, P., Austin, G., & Wolfe, D. (1991). *Reducing the system-induced trauma for child sexual abuse victims through court preparation, assessment and follow up.* London, Ontario: London Family Court Clinic. (Project No. 455-1-125)

Saywitz, K. (1989). Children's conceptions of the legal system: "Court is a place to play basketball." In S. J. Ceci, D. F. Ross, & M. P. Toglia (Eds.), *Perspectives on children's testimony* (pp. 131-157). New York: Springer Verlag.

Saywitz, K. J., & Goodman, G. S. (1996). Interviewing children in and out of court: Current research and practice. In *APSAC handbook on child maltreatment.* Chicago: APSAC.

Saywitz, K. J., & Nathanson, R. (1993). Children's testimony and their perception of stress in and out of the courtroom. *Child Abuse & Neglect, 17,* 613-622.

Saywitz, K. J., & Snyder, L. (1993). *Improving children's testimony with preparation.* New York: Guilford.

Smith, S. B. (1985). *Children's story: Sexually molested children in criminal court.* Walnut Creek, CA: Launch Press.

Sorenson, T., & Snow, B. (1991). How children tell: The process of disclosure in child sexual abuse. *Child Welfare, 70,* 3-15.

State v. Hanson, 143 WI. Statute, 2d 479, 439 N.W. 2d 505 (1989).

Stephenson, C., & Stern, P. (1992). Professional exchange: Videotaping forensic interviews: Pro or con? *APSAC Advisor, 5*(2), 5-8.

Stern, P. (1997). *Preparing and presenting expert testimony in child abuse litigation: A guide for expert witnesses and attorneys.* Thousand Oaks, CA: Sage.

Summit, R. (1983). The child sexual abuse accommodation syndrome. *Child Abuse & Neglect, 7,* 177-192.

Tobey, A., Goodman, G., Batterman-Faunce, J., Orcutt, H., & Sachsenmaier, T. (1995). *Balancing the rights of children and defendants: Accuracy and jurors' perceptions in memory and testimony in the child witness.* Thousand Oaks, CA: Sage.

Veith, V. (1994). Broken promises: A call for witness tampering sanctions in cases of child and domestic abuse. *Hamline Law Review, 18,* 181-199.

Walker, A. G. (1999). *Handbook on questioning children: A linguistic perspective* (2nd ed.). Washington, DC: American Bar Association.

Walker, A. G. (1998). *A few facts about children's language skills* (Lecture material). Falls Church, VA.

Whitcomb, D. (1992a). *Emotional effects of the court process on child sexual abuse victims.* Newton, MA: Child Victim as Witness Project, Education Development Center.

Whitcomb, D. (1992b). *Techniques for improving children's testimony* (Research Brief). Newton, MA: Child Victim as Witness Project, Education Development Center.

Whitcomb, D. (1992c). *When the victim is a child* (2nd ed). Washington, DC: National Institute of Justice.

Whitcomb, D. (1993). *Child victims as witnesses: What the research says.* Newton, MA: Education Development Center.

Wilson, K. J. (1997). *When violence begins at home: A comprehensive guide to understanding and ending domestic abuse.* Alameda, CA: Hunter House.

Index

About the Authors

Lynn M. Copen is President and Chief Executive Officer of Kid's Kourt, Inc. (kid's-kourt.com), a company that manufactures forensic court preparation products and aids for child witnesses and professionals who will educate child witnesses. She is also the Victim Witness Program Director for the Kenosha County District Attorney's Office in Keyman, Wisconsin, and has served in that role since 1981. She has experience in working with thousands of crime victims and witnesses, many of whom were severely traumatized. Prior to 1981, Ms. Copen served as a sworn law enforcement officer for the State of Wisconsin, where she investigated all types of crimes and crime scenes, interviewed hundreds of victims, and interrogated criminal suspects.

Ms. Copen was the first woman to graduate (with academic honor) from the police academy at Fort McCoy in Sparta, Wisconsin. Over the years, she has continued to study criminal behavior and victim/witness issues, has served as an expert witness at criminal trials, and has lectured on offender/victim issues at state and national conferences. In 1993, she was awarded U.S. Patent #5,201,660 for her invention, design, and implementation of a model miniature courtroom to be used as a tool for educating and preparing witnesses for courtroom and trial procedure.

Ms. Copen is a Board Certified Expert in Traumatic Stress (BCETS); a former Certified Law Enforcement Officer; and a member of the Association for the Treatment of Sexual Abusers (ATSA); National Organization of Victim Assistance (NOVA); American Professional Society on the Abuse of Children (APSAC); Wisconsin Professional Society on the Abuse of Children (WIPSAC); American Academy of Experts in Traumatic Stress (AAETS); Wisconsin Victim/Witness Professionals (WVWP); and Kenosha Domestic Abuse Intervention Project (KDAIP). She is a former member of the American Academy of Forensic Science,

175

Illinois Academy of Criminology, Minnesota Society of Clinical Pathology, and Wisconsin Attorney General's Task Force on Child Abuse.

Thomas J. Fallon is an Assistant Attorney General with the Wisconsin Department of Justice, where he is assigned to the Criminal Litigation, Antitrust, and Consumer Protection Unit. He handles a wide variety of cases, from arson to racketeering. He currently specializes in sexually violent person proceedings and child abuse prosecutions. Prior to joining the Department of Justice in January of 1993, he was an Assistant and Deputy (First Assistant) District Attorney in Kenosha County, Wisconsin. As the chief felony prosecutor, he supervised other prosecutors and specialized in child abuse and drug prosecutions. As the Deputy District Attorney, he handled the administrative and personnel matters for the office. He is author of: "The Basic Do's and Don'ts of Interviewing." *NRCCSA News*, 4(3), May/June 1995, published by the National Resource Center on Child Sexual Abuse of the National Center on Child Abuse and Neglect.